Power Maths

Year 4
Practice Book 4

CW00341648

ion

What did you do in maths in Year 4?

Draw or write what you enjoyed doing most.

This book belongs to _____ .

My class is _____ .

Series editor: Tony Staneff

Lead author: Josh Lury

Consultants (first edition): Professor Liu Jian and Professor Zhang Dan

Author team (first edition): David Board, Tim Handley, Derek Huby, Timothy Weal, Paul Wrangles and White Rose Maths (Emily Fox, Jilly Todd and Rachel Webster)

 Pearson

Contents

This looks like a good challenge!

Unit II – Decimals (2)   **6**
Make a whole   6
Partition decimals   9
Flexibly partition decimals   12
Compare decimals   15
Order decimals   18
Round to the nearest whole   21
Halves and quarters as decimals   24
End of unit check   27

Unit I2 – Money   **29**
Write money using decimals   29
Convert between pounds and pence   32
Compare amounts of money   35
Estimate with money   38
Calculate with money   41
Solve problems with money   44
End of unit check   47

Unit I3 – Time   **49**
Years, months, weeks and days   49
Hours, minutes and seconds   52
Convert between analogue and digital times 55
Convert to the 24-hour clock   58
Problem solving – convert units of time   61
End of unit check   64

Unit I4 – Geometry – angles and 2D shapes **66**
Identify angles   66
Compare and order angles   69
Triangles   72
Quadrilaterals   75

2

Polygons   78
Reason about polygons   81
Lines of symmetry   84
Complete a symmetric figure   87
End of unit check   90

Unit 15 – Statistics   **93**
Interpret charts   93
Solve problems with charts (1)   96
Solve problems with charts (2)   99
Interpret line graphs (1)   102
Interpret line graphs (2)   105
Draw line graphs   108
End of unit check   111

Unit 16 – Geometry – position and direction   **114**
Describe position   114
Describe position using coordinates   117
Plot coordinates   120
Draw 2D shapes on a grid   123
Translate on a grid   126
Describe translation on a grid   129
End of unit check   132

It's time to do some practice!

3

How to use this book

Do you remember how to use this **Practice Book**?

Use the **Textbook** first to learn how to solve this type of problem.

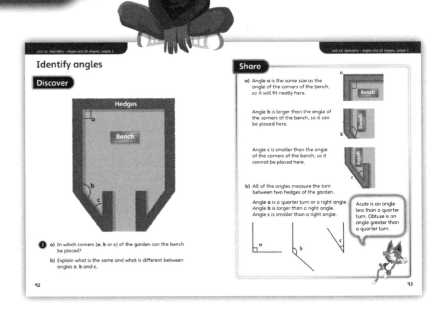

This shows you which **Textbook** page you need.

Have a go at questions by yourself using this **Practice Book**. Use what you have learnt.

Challenge questions make you think hard!

Questions with this light bulb make you think differently.

Reflect

Each lesson ends with a **Reflect** question so you can think about what you have learnt.

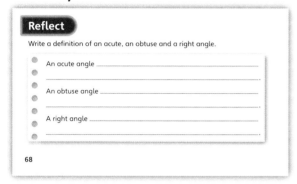

Use **My power points** at the back of this book to keep track of what you have learnt.

My journal

At the end of a unit your teacher will ask you to fill in **My journal**.

This will help you show how much you can do now that you have finished the unit.

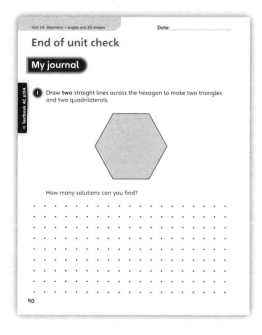

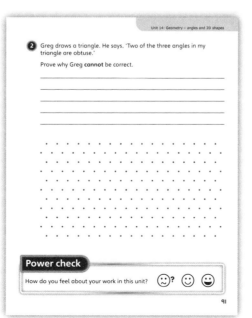

Date: _____

Make a whole

1 Use the grids to complete the additions.

a) $0·2 + 0·\boxed{} = 1$

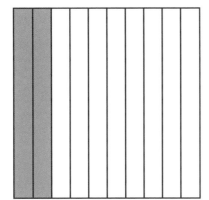

c) $0·48 + 0·\boxed{} = 1$

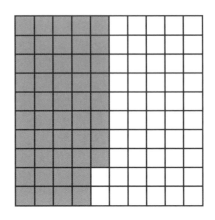

b) $0·9 + 0·\boxed{} = 1$

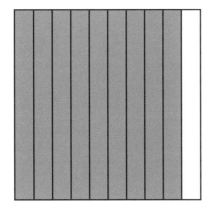

d) $0·\boxed{} + 0·\boxed{} = 1$

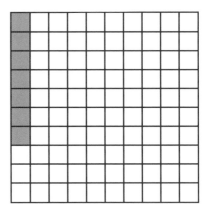

2 Work out the missing numbers. Complete the part-whole models.

a)

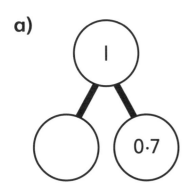

b)

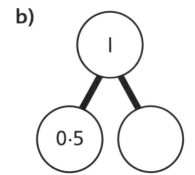

6

3 Complete the part-whole models.

a)

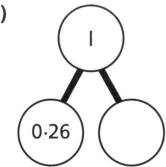

c)

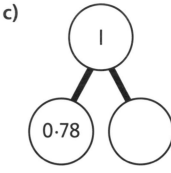

b)

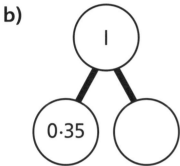

d)

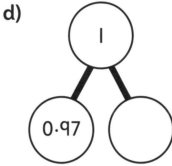

4 Complete the calculations.

a) $0 \cdot 6 + \boxed{} = 1$

e) $0 \cdot 33 + \boxed{} = 1$

b) $1 = \boxed{} + 0 \cdot 84$

f) $0 \cdot 89 + \boxed{} = 1$

c) $0 \cdot 32 + \boxed{} = 1$

g) $1 - 0 \cdot 7 = \boxed{}$

d) $\boxed{} + 0 \cdot 09 = 1$

h) $1 - 0 \cdot 34 = \boxed{}$

5 Work out the missing numbers.

a)

1	
$\boxed{}$	0·39

b)

1	
0·13	$\boxed{}$

6 Complete the calculations.

a) 0·☐3 + 0·7☐ = 1

b) 0·☐5 + 0·2☐ = 1

c) 0·☐ + 0·☐8 = 1

d) 0·3☐ + 0·☐ = 1

e) 0·3☐ + 0·☐ = 1

f) 0·3☐ + 0·☐ = 1

7 Use the number cards to make each row and column add up to 1 whole.

0·3 0·5 0·6 0·1 0·2

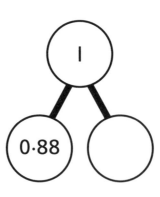

Reflect

Max says, '0·22 is the missing value.'

Explain why Max is not correct.

1 → 0·88, ☐

_____

_____

_____

8

Partition decimals

1 What numbers are shown on the place value grids?

a)
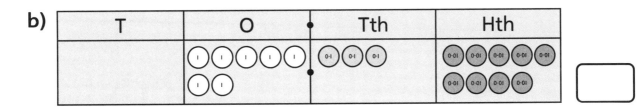

b)
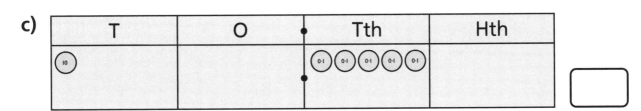

c)

T	O	Tth	Hth
10		0·1 0·1 0·1 0·1 0·1	

2 Complete the part-whole models.

a)
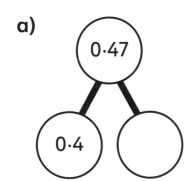

c)
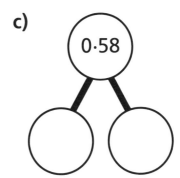

b)
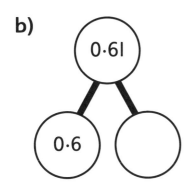

d)
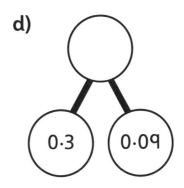

9

3 Complete the bar model.

3·49		
3	☐	0·09

4 Complete the part-whole models.

a)
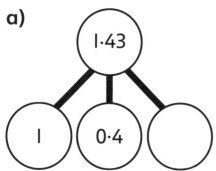

b)
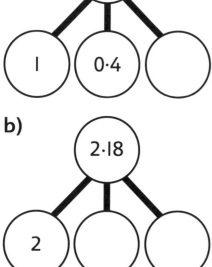

c)
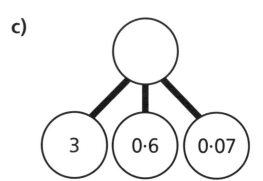

d)
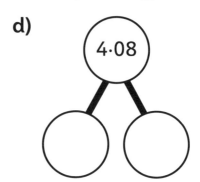

5 Complete the table.

a)	7 ones + 2 tenths + 1 hundredth	7·☐
b)	2 tens + 9 _____ + 3 tenths + 4 _____	☐9·☐4
c)	1 ten + 7 ones + 1 hundredth	☐☐·☐
d)	5 tenths + 3 hundredths	☐·☐

6 Complete the additions.

a) $0.65 = 0.6 + \boxed{}$

e) $\boxed{} = 0.01 + 0.6$

b) $0.39 = 0.3 + \boxed{}$

f) $2.38 = 2 + 0.3 + \boxed{}$

c) $0.87 = 0.07 + \boxed{}$

g) $3.15 = 3 + \boxed{} + 0.05$

d) $\boxed{} = 0.6 + 0.01$

h) $\boxed{} = 1 + 0.9 + 0.02$

7 Mo, Emma and Danny are playing a number game. Each child gives one clue. Draw lines to show which number matches each child.

CHALLENGE

8·24   4·24   4·27

My number has 2 tenths.

My number has the same quantity of ones and hundredths.

My number has 4 hundredths.

Mo   Emma   Danny

Reflect

Write down a decimal and ask a partner to partition it.

_____

_____

11

Date: _____

Flexibly partition decimals

1 Complete the part-whole models.

a)

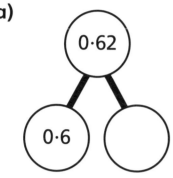

c)

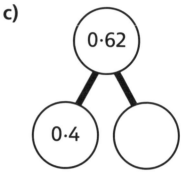

b)

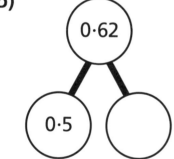

d)

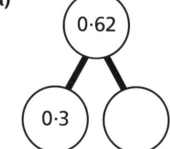

Textbook 4C p16

2 Complete the partitions.

a)

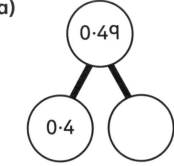

c)

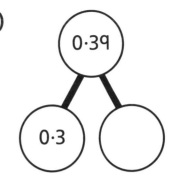

b)

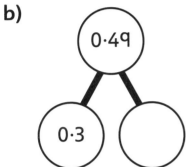

d)

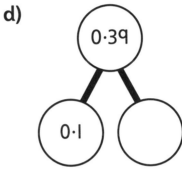

3 Complete the different partitions of 2·35.

Use the counters to help you.

a)

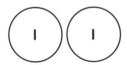 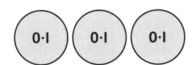 

$2 \cdot 35 = 2 + \boxed{} + \boxed{}$

b)

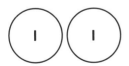  

$2 \cdot 35 = 2 + 0 \cdot 2 + \boxed{}$

13

4 Complete the partitions.

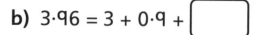
CHALLENGE

a) $0.74 = 0.7 + \boxed{}$

b) $3.96 = 3 + 0.9 + \boxed{}$

$0.74 = 0.6 + \boxed{}$

$3.96 = 1 + 2.9 + \boxed{}$

$0.74 = 0.5 + \boxed{}$

$3.96 = 3 + 0.4 + \boxed{}$

$0.74 = 0.3 + \boxed{}$

$3.96 = 2 + 1.9 + \boxed{}$

$0.74 = 0.2 + \boxed{}$

$3.96 = 3 + 0.8 + \boxed{}$

Reflect

Choose one of these numbers. How many ways can you partition it?

$\boxed{0.43}$ $\boxed{5.26}$

Date: _____

Compare decimals

1 Write < or > to compare the number.

a)

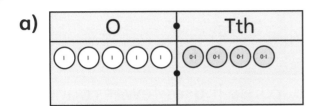 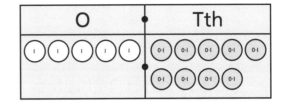

b)

 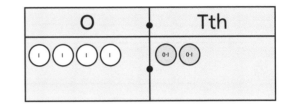

2 Circle the smaller number in each pair.

a) 0·65   0·36   d) 6·85   6·81

b) 1·7   1·9   e) 13·8   38·1

c) 1·35   1·46

3 Circle the greater number in each pair

a) 0·78   0·75   c) 17·8   30·1

b) 3·99   5·58   d) 11·5   7·53

→ Textbook 4C p20

4 Richard makes two numbers.

O		Tth	Hth
① ① ①		⓪·¹ ⓪·¹	⓪·⁰¹

O		Tth	Hth
① ① ①			⓪·⁰¹ ⓪·⁰¹ ⓪·⁰¹ ⓪·⁰¹ ⓪·⁰¹ ⓪·⁰¹ ⓪·⁰¹

He says that 3·21 is less than 3·07 because it uses fewer counters.
Explain why Richard is not correct.

_____

_____

5 Complete each sentence using <, > or =.

a) 0·8 ◯ 0·3

b) 0·35 ◯ 0·45

c) 4·56 ◯ 4·72

d) 12·9 ◯ 18·7

e) 9·45 ◯ 9·05

f) 3·18 ◯ 3·12

g) 26·39 ◯ 27·49

h) 120·26 ◯ 120·26

i) 3 tenths + 5 hundredths ◯ 5 tenths and 4 hundredths

6 Write down three numbers between 1·65 and 1·72.

7 Reena and Ambika have each represented a decimal.

O		Tth	Hth
	•	0·1 0·1 0·1	0·01 0·01

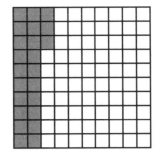

Reena   Ambika

Who has made the smaller number? _____

Discuss your answer with a partner.

8 Insert numbers to make the statements correct.
Find three different answers for each question.

CHALLENGE

a) 6·74 > 6·☐4

 6·74 > 6·☐4

 6·74 > 6·☐4

b) 2·☐3 < 2·3☐

 2·☐3 < 2·3☐

 2·☐3 < 2·3☐

Reflect

Explain to a partner how to compare two decimals.

Date: _____

Order decimals

 Put these numbers in order starting with the smallest.

| 7·2 | | 6·7 | | 7·9 |

O	Tth
7	2

O	Tth
6	7

O	Tth
7	9

Smallest ⬚ , ⬚ , ⬚ Greatest

 Put the numbers in order from smallest to greatest.

| 0·43 | | 0·25 | | 0·09 |

Smallest ⬚ , ⬚ , ⬚ Greatest

3 **a)** Circle the place value grid which shows the greatest number.

T	O	Tth	Hth
1	0	0	7

T	O	Tth	Hth
1	0	7	9

T	O	Tth	Hth
1	0	9	7

T	O	Tth	Hth
1	0	0	9

b) Order the numbers from greatest to smallest.

 , , ,

4 **a)** Put the numbers in order starting with the smallest.

| 27·24 | 72·45 | 7·42 | 27·48 |

Smallest ⬚ , ⬚ , ⬚ , ⬚ Greatest

b) Put the numbers in order starting with the greatest.

| 4·53 | 4·59 | 5·94 | 5·49 |

Greatest ⬚ , ⬚ , ⬚ , ⬚ Smallest

5 Circle the child who is incorrect. Discuss your answer with a partner.

The numbers are in descending order.

The numbers are ordered most to least.

The numbers are ordered smallest to greatest.

The numbers are ordered greatest to smallest.

Reena   Kate   Aki   Max

12·99   12·09   9·12

6 Five children compete in a 100 m race. The results are shown in the table.

Name	Time (in seconds)
Mo	28·02
Isla	28·42
Amelia	27·79
Ebo	29·53
Lee	28·24

a) Write the times from smallest to greatest.

b) Who was the fastest?

_____

c) Who was the slowest?

_____

7 Put a digit in each box so the numbers are in ascending order.

CHALLENGE

4·0☐, 4·☐9, ☐·01, ☐·☐☐

Reflect

Convince a partner that 0·62 < 0·65 < 0·71.

_____

_____

_____

Round to the nearest whole

 a) Round 2·7 to the nearest whole number.

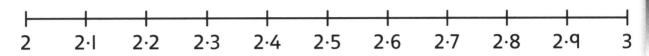

2   2·1   2·2   2·3   2·4   2·5   2·6   2·7   2·8   2·9   3

2·7 is between ☐ and ☐.

2·7 rounded to the nearest whole number is ☐.

b) Round 10·3 to the nearest whole number.

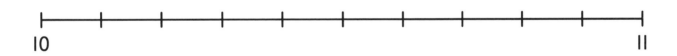

10   11

10·3 is between ☐ and ☐.

10·3 rounded to the nearest whole number is ☐.

c) Round 28·5 to the nearest whole number.

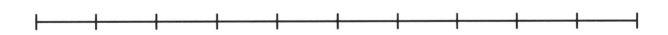

28·5 is between ☐ and ☐.

28·5 rounded to the nearest whole number is ☐.

Textbook 4C p28

2 Complete the previous and next whole numbers.

Previous whole number   Next whole number

Previous	Number	Next
☐	1·8	☐
☐	2·5	☐
☐	5·4	☐
☐	12·9	☐
☐	65·3	☐

3 Round these numbers to the nearest whole number.

a) 5·4 ☐   e) 50·8 ☐

b) 12·9 ☐   f) 150·5 ☐

c) 65·3 ☐   g) 400·1 ☐

d) 0·4 ☐   h) 89·6 ☐

4 Which of these cannot be Luis's number?
Explain your answer.

55·2   54·8   54·5   55·5   55·1

> I rounded a number to the nearest whole number. The answer is 55.

Luis

_____

_____

_____

5 Complete the sentences.

a) 4·9 rounded to the nearest _____ is 5.

b) ☐·5 rounded to the nearest whole number is 9.

c) 12·☐ rounded to the nearest whole number is 12.

d) ☐·☐ rounded to the nearest whole number is 23.

6 Use the number cards to make as many numbers as you can with 1 decimal place. All your numbers must round to 80 as the nearest whole number.

CHALLENGE

| 0 | 3 | 4 |
| 5 | 7 | 8 |

Reflect

Explain how to use the tenths digit to help you round 43·6 to the nearest whole number.

_____

_____

_____

Date: _____

Halves and quarters as decimals

1 Use the grids to help you write these decimals as fractions.

a) $0 \cdot 25 = \dfrac{\boxed{}}{\boxed{}}$

b) $0 \cdot 50 = \dfrac{\boxed{}}{\boxed{}}$

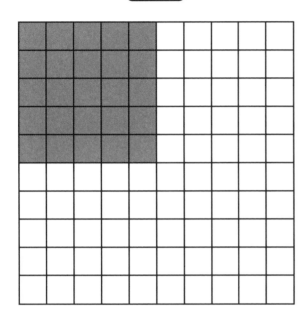
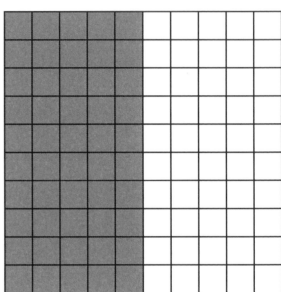

2 Alex is working out the decimal equivalent of $\frac{3}{4}$.

Her answer is $\frac{3}{4} = 3 \cdot 4$.

a) Shade in the hundredths grid to show Alex is incorrect.

b) What is the correct answer?

$\frac{3}{4} = \boxed{}$

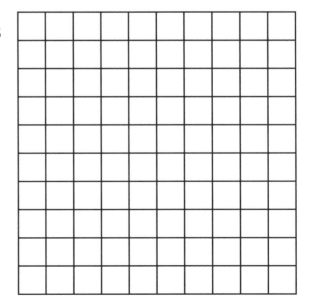

3 Use the number lines to complete the decimal equivalents.

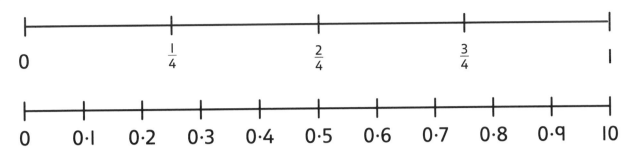

a) $\frac{1}{4}$ = [   ]   c) $\frac{3}{4}$ = [   ]

b) $\frac{2}{4}$ = [   ]   d) $\frac{1}{2}$ = [   ]

4 a) Shade in 0·25 of this shape.

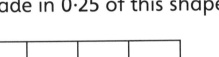

> Use your knowledge of equivalent fractions to help you shade in the shapes.

b) Shade in 0·5 of this shape.

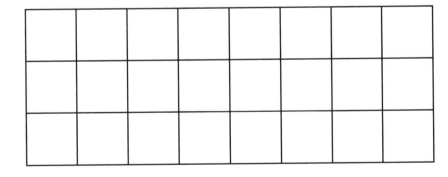

c) Shade in 0·75 of this shape.

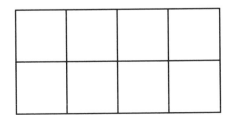

5 Zac has 0·5 of the apples. Emma has $\frac{1}{2}$ of the apples.

I think that Zac has 5 apples and Emma 2 apples.

Olivia

Zac and Emma have the same number of apples.

Bella

Who is correct, Olivia or Bella? Explain your answer to a partner.

6 Complete the table.

CHALLENGE

Decimal	Fraction
0·75	
1·25	
	$1\frac{1}{2}$
	$2\frac{1}{4}$
3·5	
4·75	

Reflect

Use the grid to show that $\frac{3}{4}$ is equal to 0·75. Explain your answer below.

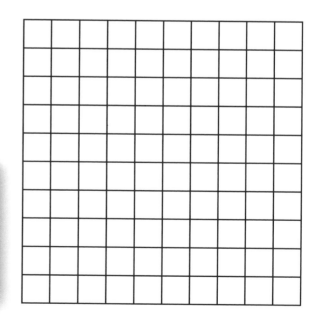

_____

_____

_____

Date: _____

End of unit check

My journal

| 7·2 | 7·20 | 0·27 |

What is the same about these numbers?

_____

_____

_____

_____

What is different about these numbers?

_____

_____

_____

_____

These words might help you.

tenths   hundredths

decimal   place value

Power check

How do you feel about your work in this unit?

↓ Textbook 4C p36

Power puzzle

Join pairs that total 1. One has been done for you. Use a ruler.

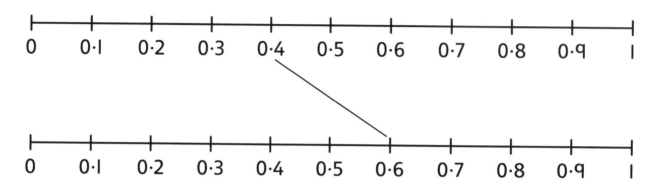

Now do the same with these two lines.

What patterns do you notice?

I will try my own number line patterns like this.

I wonder if I could label my lines in steps of 0·05.

Write money using decimals

↓ Textbook 4C p40

1 How much money is shown? Write your answer in pounds as a decimal.

a)

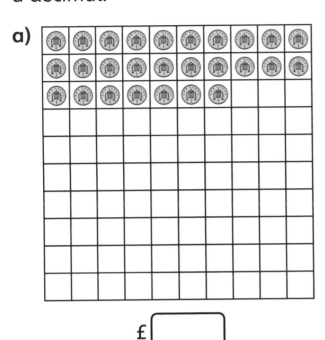

£ [ ]

b)

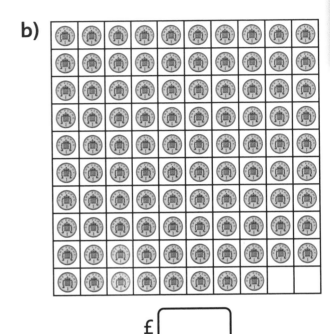

£ [ ]

2 How much money is here?

a)

[ ] p = £ [ ]

b)

[ ] p = £ [ ]

29

3 How much money is in each box?

Write your answer in pounds.

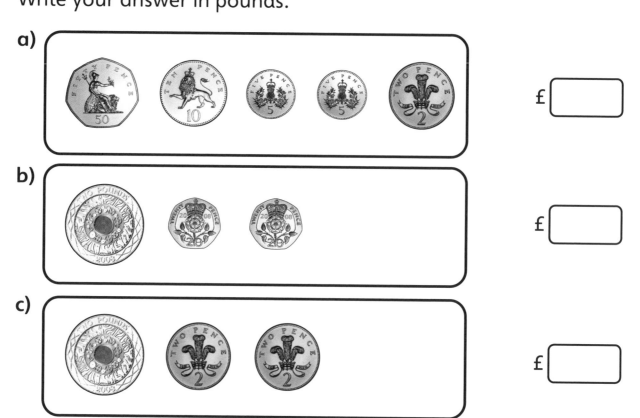

a) £ ☐

b) £ ☐

c) £ ☐

4 **a)** Circle £0·27.

b) Circle £1·30.

c) Circle £1·03.

Key 1p 2p 5p 10p 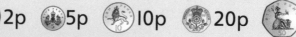20p 50p £1 ●£2

5 Aki has some money in his hand.

Aki writes this as £4·3.

Is Aki correct? If not, explain his mistake.

_____

_____

_____

_____

6 Complete the table. Write your answers in pence.

$\frac{3}{10}$ of £1	$\frac{3}{100}$ of £1	$\frac{73}{100}$ of £1	$\frac{9}{10}$ of £1	$\frac{90}{100}$ of £1
30p				

Reflect

What is the same and what is different about £1·30 and £1·03?

_____
_____
_____
_____
_____

 £5   £10   £20   £50

Date: _____

Convert between pounds and pence

1 Write each amount in pence.
Then write it as a decimal in pounds.

a)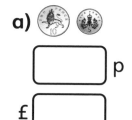

☐ p

£ ☐

b)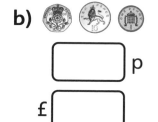

☐ p

£ ☐

c)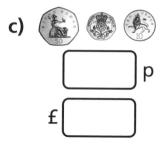

☐ p

£ ☐

2 Write each amount in pence, then convert it into pounds and write it as a decimal.

a)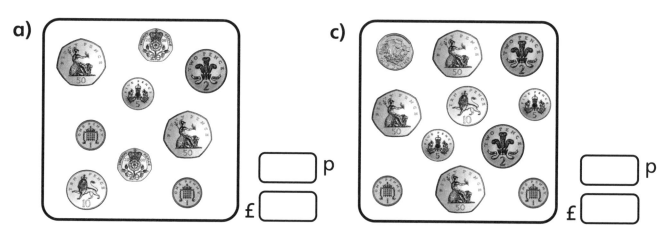

☐ p

£ ☐

b)

☐ p

£ ☐

c)

☐ p

£ ☐

d)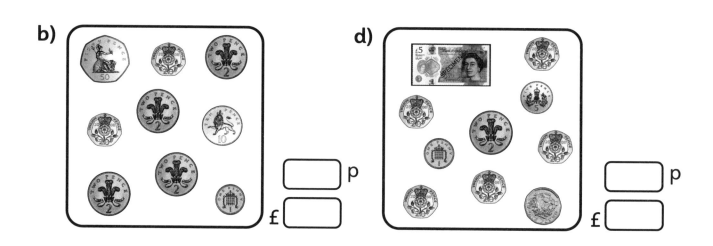

☐ p

£ ☐

32

Key 1p 2p 5p 10p 20p  50p £1 £2

3 **a)** Circle £8·72.

b) Circle £12·18.

4 Write the totals.

a) £1 + 50p + 20p + 20p + 5p + 2p = £ ⬚

b) £1 + £1 + £1 + 50p + 50p + 5p + 1p = £ ⬚

c) 20p + £1 + 50p + 10p + 50p + 10p = £ ⬚

5 Complete the following equivalents.

a) 258p = £ ⬚

b) 370p = £ ⬚

c) 408p = £ ⬚

d) 1,257p = £ ⬚

e) £1·18 = ⬚ p

f) £8·95 = ⬚ p

g) ⬚ p = £2·09

h) ⬚ p = £2·90

i) £11·15 = ⬚ p

j) £9 = ⬚ p

 £5 £10 £20 £50

6 Four boxes contain different amounts of money.

- Box A contains 300p.
- Box B contains 10 times as much as Box A.
- Box C contains 10p more than Box A.
- Box D contains 100p less than Box B.

How much money is in each box?

Write your answers in pounds.

Box A = £ [ ]   Box B = £ [ ]   Box C = £ [ ]   Box D = £ [ ]

Reflect

Describe three ways you can write how much money there is in total.

_____

_____

Key 1p 2p 5p 10p 20p 50p £1 £2

Compare amounts of money

1 **a)** Circle the least expensive item.

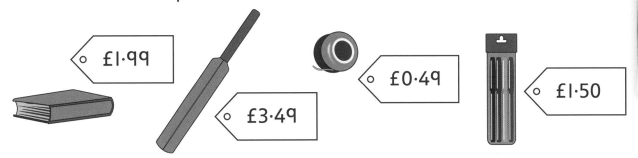

£1·99

£3·49

£0·49

£1·50

Explain how you know.

_____

_____

b) Circle the most expensive item.

498p

4 pounds 89 pence

£0·98

849 pence

Explain how you worked this out.

_____

_____

2 Circle all the items you could buy with a £5 note.

349 pence

£0·69

£6·09

I pound 95 pence

3 Complete each statement with a <, > or = sign.

a) 72p ◯ 50p   £2 ◯ £8

   72p ◯ 500p   £2 ◯ 200p

   72p ◯ 5p   £2 ◯ £2·05

   72p ◯ £5   £2 ◯ 195p

b) Seven pounds eighty pence ◯ £7·09

   £5·99 ◯ six pounds

4 Put these amounts in order from the smallest to the greatest.

a) £5·25   255 pence   £2·05   £0·25

_____

b) 408 pence   £0·84   £8·40   £8·04

_____

5 Put these amounts in order from the greatest to the smallest.

a) 98 pence   eight pounds ninety pence   £0·89   £0·99

_____

_____

b) 1 pound 1 pence   £0·01   11 pounds   £1·11   110 pence

_____

Key 1p 2p 5p 10p 20p 50p ◯£1 ◯£2

6 Use these digits to make the statements true. | 5 | 6 | 8 | 9 |

a) £4·75 > £4·☐2

c) £475 > £4☐5

b) £47·50 < £4☐·50

d) £0·47 < £0·☐2

7 Use the clues to match the child to the correct money bag. **CHALLENGE**

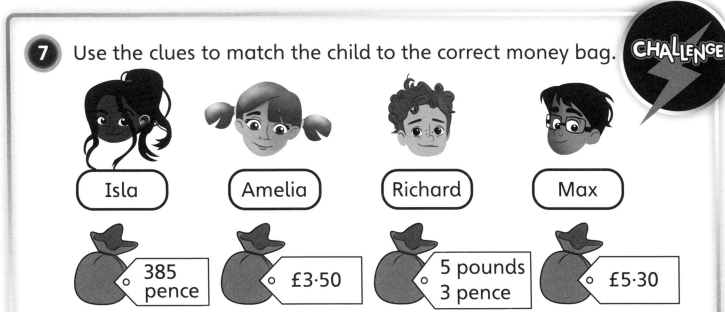

Isla   Amelia   Richard   Max

385 pence   £3·50   5 pounds 3 pence   £5·30

Clues:
- Amelia has the greatest amount of money.
- Richard and Isla have the same amount of pounds.
- Richard has more money than Isla.

Reflect

Isla says, '257 pence is greater than 3 pounds as 257 > 3.'

Do you agree with Isla? Explain why or why not.

_____

_____

 £5   £10   £20   £50

Date: _____

Estimate with money

1 Match the prices to the best estimate.

| o £1·99 | o £0·95 | o £2·01 | o £2·98 | o £1·90 |

$£1$ $£2$ $£3$ $£4$

2 Write the best estimate for each item.

o £1·88 [ ]

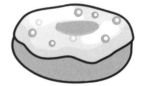

o £1·49 [ ]

o £2·95 [ ]

o £9·75 [ ]

38

Key 1p 2p 5p 10p 20p 50p £1 £2

3 **a)** Estimate the total cost of these items.

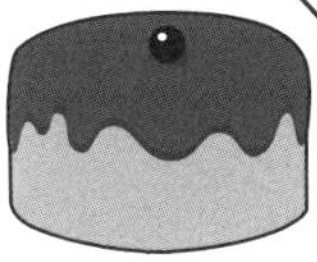

£1·89

£0·95

£3·75

Estimate £ ⬚

b) Explain whether you have made an over or an under estimate.

_____

_____

4 Estimate the total cost of these items.
Show your estimates clearly.

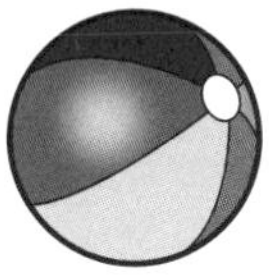

£4·95    £5·49    £5·92    £4·22 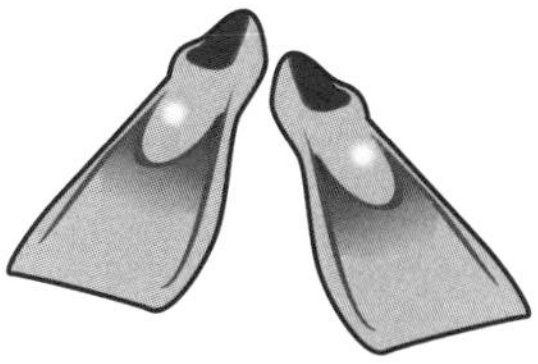   £5·50

Estimate £ ⬚

 £5   £10   £20  £50

5 Sofia wants to buy a car costing £7,959.

She has saved £1,875.

Estimate how much more money Sofia needs to save.

I estimate Sofia needs to save £ [ ] .

6 Lexi has £20. She wants to buy some items with these prices.

CHALLENGE

£5·43   £2·07   £6·30   £4·49   £2·26

She finds the nearest whole pound for each price.
'I estimate the total to be £19, so I have enough money.'
Why might Lexi not be correct?

_____

_____

Reflect

Write three different amounts that you would estimate as £10.
Write three different amounts that you would estimate as £4·50.

_____

_____

Key 1p 2p 5p 10p 20p 50p £1 £2

Date: _____

Calculate with money

1 **a)** How much money does Max have?

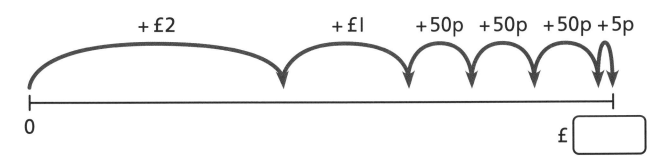

+£2   +£1   +50p +50p +50p +5p

0

£ ☐

b) How much money does Olivia have?

Olivia has £ ☐ and ☐ p.

c) How much money do Max and Olivia have altogether?

Max and Olivia have £ ☐ in total.

 £5   £10   £20   £50

Textbook 4C p56

2 Jamilla buys these items for lunch.

How much does she spend in total?

£1·59

£2·45

3 Work out the totals.

a) £2·48 + £30·08 =

b) 72p and £4·95 =

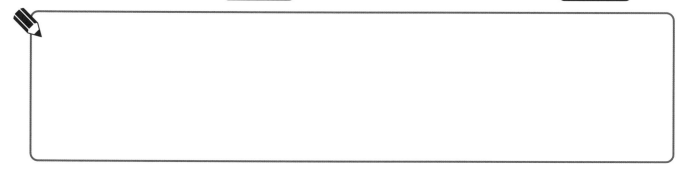

4 Reena spends £2·85 on a large birthday balloon.

She pays with a £5 note.

How much change does she get from £5?

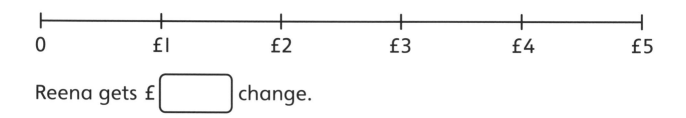

0   £1   £2   £3   £4   £5

Reena gets £ ☐ change.

Key 1p 2p 5p 10p 20p 50p £1 £2

5 Luis spends £6·35. How much change would he get from a £10 note?

6 Lexi buys a DVD and a basketball using a £20 note and a £5 note.

What is the minimum number of coins she will get in her change?

Dinosuar World

£13·35

£7·40

CHALLENGE

Reflect

Prove Mo will get some change from a £5 note if he buys three items costing £2·55, 70p and £1·68.

  £5   £10    £20   £50

Date: _____

Solve problems with money

1 A banana costs 84p.

Andy buys 5 bananas.

He pays with a £5 note.

How much change does Andy get?

Andy gets £ ⬚ change.

2 Aki buys 8 packs of stickers.

He pays with a £10 note.

Aki receives £3·52 change.

a) Explain how you know a pack of stickers costs less than £1.

_____

_____

b) How much does one pack of stickers cost?

A pack of stickers costs £ ⬚ .

Remember, you need to change the amount into pence first.

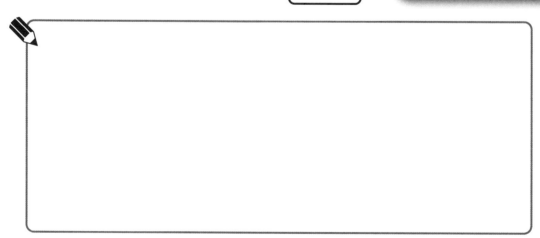

Key 1p 2p 5p 10p 20p 50p £1 £2

3 Is it cheaper to pay for 6 throws for £1·20 or 6 throws at 25p per throw?

> 6 throws for £1·20 or 25 pence a throw.

It is cheaper to_____

because_____ .

4 Sofia can travel to work using two taxi companies.

> **POWER CABS**
> £3 first km and then
> 40p for each km after

> **AI CARS**
> 70p for each km
> travelled

Sofia wants to travel 9 km to work.

Which taxi company is less expensive for Sofia's journey?

Show your working.

The less expensive taxi company for Sofia is _____ .

5 Work out the missing numbers.

£2·☐ + £☐·75 = £8·42

6 Amelia wants to buy 5 buns.

Amelia says it is cheaper to buy the bag of buns, because each bun costs 50p.

Is Amelia correct? _____

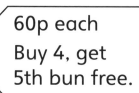

60p each

Buy 4, get 5th bun free.

CHALLENGE

£2·50

Reflect

A single bread roll costs 55p.
It is cheaper to buy a pack of 4 bread rolls than to buy 4 single rolls.
How much would you charge for the pack of 4 rolls? Explain why.

_____

_____

Key 1p 2p 5p 10p 20p 50p £1 £2

End of unit check

My journal

Ebo wants to add £1·34 and 72p.

Lexi says, 'You can't add these amounts as they are different units.'

Mo says, 'Lexi is right and we do not know how to add decimals yet.'

Explain to Ebo how he could add these amounts.

_____

_____

_____

_____

_____

_____

_____

Power check

How do you feel about your work in this unit?

 £5   £10   £20    £50

Power puzzle

1 A kettle costs twice as much as a toaster.

The toaster and kettle cost £72 in total.

How much does each item cost?

A toaster costs £⬚.

A kettle costs £⬚.

£72

2 A laptop costs 5 times as much as a radio.

The laptop is £340 more than the radio.

How much does the radio cost?

The radio costs £⬚.

3 A pair of speakers costs 3 times as much as a pair of headphones.

A camera costs £36 more than the pair of speakers.

The total cost of the 3 items is £155.

How much does each item cost?

A pair of speakers costs £⬚.

A pair of headphones costs £⬚.

A camera costs £⬚.

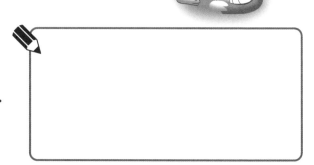

Can you put all the objects in order, starting with the least expensive?

Years, months, weeks and days

1 Convert the units of time. Use the bar models to help you.

a)

21 days		
☐ days	☐ days	☐ days

$21 \div 7 = $ ☐ weeks

The orange juice should be used within ☐ weeks.

b)

3 weeks and 5 days

1 week	1 week	1 week	5 days
☐ days	☐ days	☐ days	☐ days

☐ days

The parcel should be delivered in ☐ days.

c)

Suitable for children over 36 months.

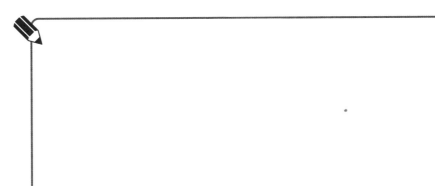

The toy is suitable for children over ☐ years old.

2 Draw lines to match the lengths of time.

4 years	about 30 weeks
12 weeks	730 days
2 years	48 days
6 weeks 6 days	48 months
7 months	84 days

3 How many weeks are 53 days?

There are 7 days in a week. 53 × 7 equals 371 weeks.

Lee

Explain the mistake that Lee has made.

_____

_____

_____

4 Complete the calculations.

a) 5 weeks + 13 days = 6 weeks ☐ days

b) 38 months − 2 years = ☐ months

5 Complete the sentences.

To find the number of ...

months in a number of years, _____multiply_____ by ☐.

years in a number of months, _____ by ☐.

days in a number of weeks, _____ by ☐.

weeks in a number of days, _____ by ☐.

6 How old are you in years, weeks and days?

☐ years, ☐ weeks and ☐ days.

How many days old are you?

CHALLENGE

I am ☐ days old.

Reflect

A baby is 20 months old. How long ago (in years and months) was it born?

I can find the answer by _____

_____

_____.

Date: _____

Hours, minutes and seconds

1. A space shuttle is counting down to take off.

   These timers show the time left in different ways.

   Work out the missing times.

   a)

   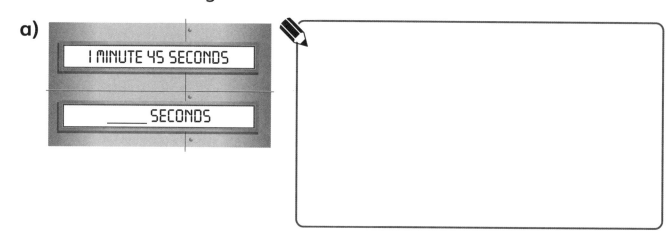

   b)

   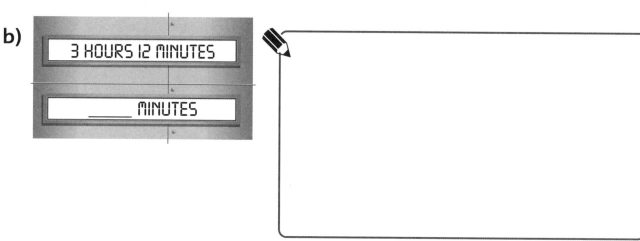

   c)

2 Show how you can use the 6 times-table to help convert times.

a) 1 × 6 = ☐   1 × 60 = ☐   1 hour = ☐ minutes

b) 2 × 6 = ☐   2 × 60 = ☐   ☐ hours = ☐ minutes

c) 3 × 6 = ☐   3 × 60 = ☐   ☐ hours = ☐ minutes

d) 4 × 6 = ☐   4 × 60 = ☐   ☐ hours = ☐ minutes

e) 10 × 6 = ☐   10 × 60 = ☐   ☐ hours = ☐ minutes

3 Use subtraction to find the length of each film in hours and minutes.

Film	Length (minutes)
Lift Off!	135
Escape from Saturn	95
Star Voyager	145

The first film has been done for you.

a) Lift Off!

   135 minutes
 − 60 minutes (1 hour)
 ───────────
=   75 minutes
 − 60 minutes (1 hour)
 ───────────
=   15 minutes

= 2 hours and
 15 minutes

b) Escape from Saturn

c) Star Voyager

4 The winner of the London Marathon finished in 2 hours and 5 minutes.

Ella's dad completed the race in 4 hours and 15 minutes.

How many minutes after the winner did Ella's dad finish the race?

5 Tom's kitchen tap drips once every second.

He puts a bowl underneath it to catch the water.

How many drops will be in the bowl after 1 hour?

Show your working.

CHALLENGE

Reflect

Discuss with a partner how to work out the number of hours and minutes in 152 minutes.

Date: _____

Convert between analogue and digital times

1 Draw these digital times on the analogue clocks.

a) 1:30 am

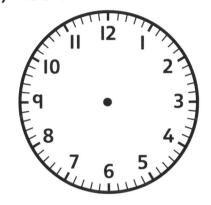

d) 7:20 pm

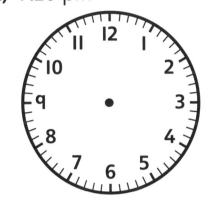

b) 2:45 pm

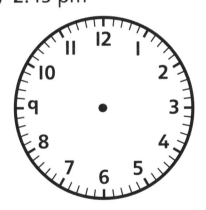

e) 11:58 am

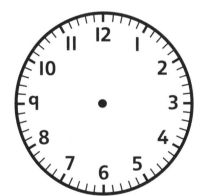

c) 3:53 pm

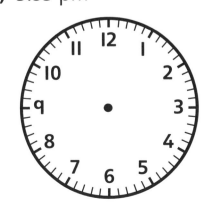

f) 8:40 pm

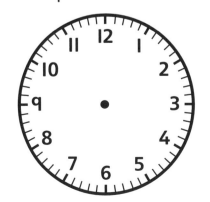

2 Here are some extracts from a spy's diary. Fill in each time on the analogue and digital clocks. Remember to write am or pm.

a) Catch the plane at 12 minutes past 2 in the morning.

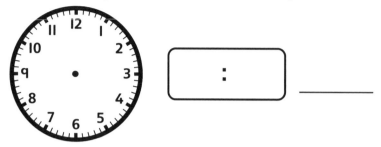

b) Meet Agent X at quarter to 1 in the afternoon.

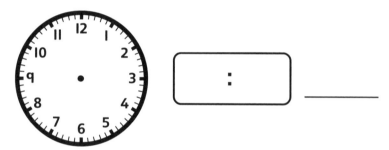

c) Crack the code by 17 minutes past 6 in the evening.

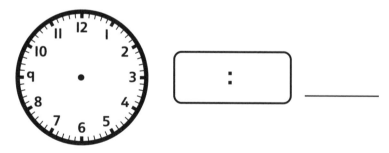

3 Kate says, 'It is quarter to 10. My digital clock time has the digit 9 in it. My analogue clock shows the minute hand pointing to the number 9, but they both represent different things!'

Discuss with a partner what the 9 means on each clock.

4 It is the afternoon. A digital time contains a 3, a 6 and a 5.

What are four possible times it could be?

Convert each time into an analogue time.

Reflect

Explain how to convert an analogue 12-hour time into a digital time.

To convert from analogue into digital, I would _____

_____

_____ .

Date: _____

Convert to the 24-hour clock

1 What would each time look like on an analogue and a 24-hour digital clock?

a) 1:05 am

b) 7 o'clock in the evening

c) 11:41 pm

d) 8:28 am

e) 2 minutes past midnight

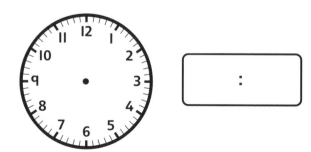

2 Convert these 24-hour digital times into 12-hour digital times. Write am or pm after the time.

a) 13:42 ☐ : ☐ _____

b) 15:30 ☐ : ☐ _____

c) 09:40 ☐ : ☐ _____

d) 20:48 ☐ : ☐ _____

e) 22:11 ☐ : ☐ _____

f) 00:00 ☐ : ☐ _____

3 These 24-hour times have been written incorrectly.

Write each time correctly. Explain the mistakes to your partner.

a) 3:42 ☐ : ☐

b) 15:42 pm ☐ : ☐

4 Aki is going shopping. His watch shows 24-hour times.

His mum says, 'It is now 2:17 pm. I will meet you outside the sports shop in an hour and a half.'

What time will Aki's watch show when he has to meet his mum?

Aki's watch will show ☐ : ☐ .

5 Write down ten 24-hour times where the four digits add up to 8 each time.

Convert your times into 12-hour times.

For example, 05:21 → 5:21 am

	24-hour time	12-hour time
1		
2		
3		
4		
5		

	24-hour time	12-hour time
6		
7		
8		
q		
10		

Reflect

Explain how to convert between 12-hour and 24-hour times.

Date: _____

Problem solving – convert units of time

1 Two teams of explorers raced each other to the top of a mountain.

They completed four different stages until they reached the top.

This is a record of their climbs.

Team	Stage 1	Stage 2	Stage 3	Stage 4
Team A	1 week 2 days	2 weeks	1 week 4 days	2 weeks 1 day
Team B	10 days	13 days	11 days	17 days

a) Who completed Stage 1 first?

Team _____ was the first to complete Stage 1. It took ⬜ days.

b) How long did it take Team B to complete Stages 1 and 2 altogether?

It took ⬜ weeks and ⬜ days altogether for Team B to complete Stages 1 and 2.

c) Which team reached the summit first? By how many days?

Show your working.

Team _____ reached the summit ⬜ days before Team _____ .

2 The table shows some athletics records. Convert the times into a different unit of measurement.

Event	Record	Convert to			
Men's 800 m	100 seconds	☐ minutes	☐ seconds		
Women's 1,500 m	230 seconds	☐ minutes	☐ seconds		
Men's 3,000 m	440 seconds	☐ minutes	☐ seconds		
Women's 20 km walk	83 minutes	☐ hours	☐ minutes		
Men's 50 km walk	212 minutes	☐ hours	☐ minutes		

Show your working.

3 The classroom clock is analogue. Zac's digital watch shows 24-hour times.

It is twenty to 3 in the afternoon.

What do the clock and the watch look like?

62

4 Here is information about the ages of four children.

Abdul	Ben	Cerys	Dan
24 months	I year I0 months	3 months older than Ben	4 months younger than Cerys

Write the children's names in order from youngest to oldest.

5 A bus takes 95 minutes to travel from the bus station to the retail park. It arrives at the retail park at 14:02. What time did it leave the bus station?

The bus left the bus station at ☐ : ☐ .

Reflect

Explain to a partner how you would convert I08 months into years.

Date: _____

End of unit check

Textbook 4C p88

My journal

How long have you been alive? Is this more, equal to or less than 100 months?

Show your working.

I know I have been alive more / the same as / fewer than 100 months

because _____

_____

_____

Keywords: convert, months, years, units

Power check

How do you feel about your work in this unit?

Power puzzle

Inside this grid, there is one time that does not have an equal pair.

Which one is it?

Shade each pair in a different colour to help you spot the odd time out.

If you are working with a partner, take it in turns to shade a pair until you are left with the odd one out.

06:56	3 hours 46 minutes	60 months	(clock showing 6:00)	8 weeks 4 days
01:02	226 minutes	5 years	17:56	4 years 11 months
(clock showing 1:02)	60 days	6:56 am	59 months	13:10

Make your own puzzle for a partner to solve. Remember that each time must be part of a pair – apart from one!

65

Date: _____

Identify angles

1 **a)** Tick the acute angles.

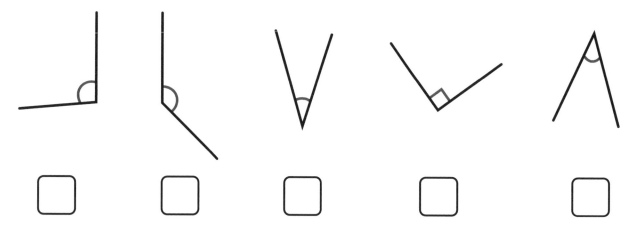

b) Tick the right angles.

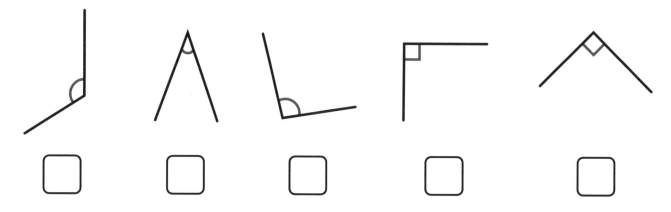

c) Tick the obtuse angles.

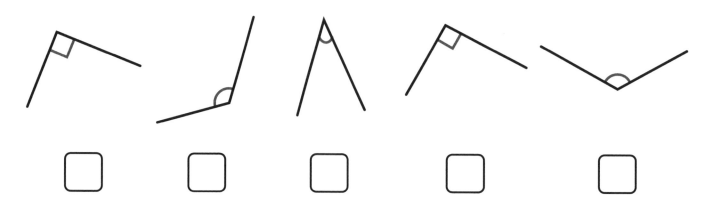

2 Draw a right angle, an acute angle and an obtuse angle.

3 Tick the shape which is in the wrong place.

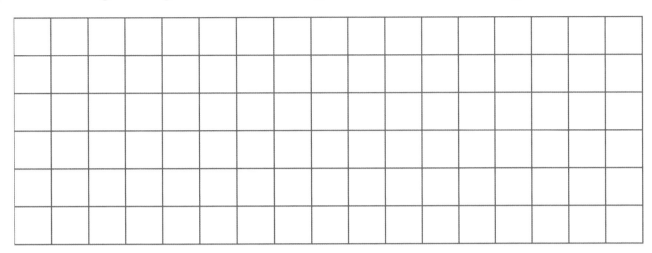

	Shapes with an acute angle	Shapes without an acute angle
Shapes with an obtuse angle		
Shapes without an obtuse angle		

4 Philippa is standing in the middle of the field.
Circle the objects she would be facing if she turned an
obtuse angle in either direction.

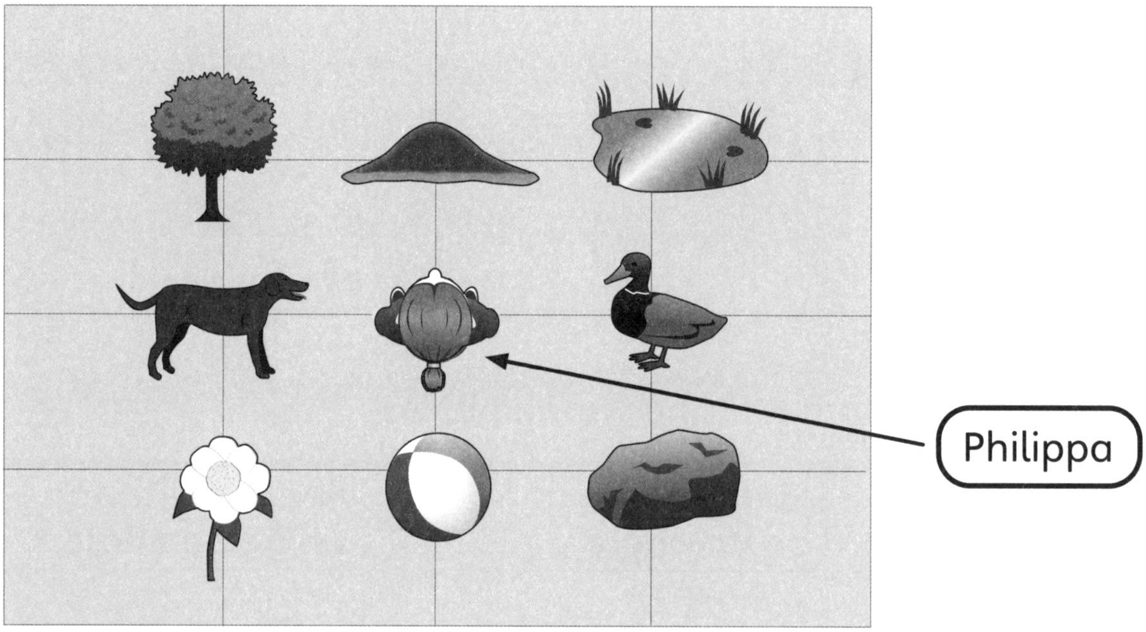

CHALLENGE

Philippa

Reflect

Write a definition of an acute, an obtuse and a right angle.

An acute angle _____
_____.

An obtuse angle _____
_____.

A right angle _____
_____.

Compare and order angles

 a) Circle the smallest angle.

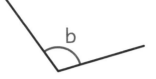

b) Circle the largest angle.

c) Circle the largest angle.

2 Compare and order these angles from greatest to smallest.

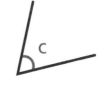

Greatest   Smallest

69

3 **a)** Compare and order these angles from smallest to greatest.

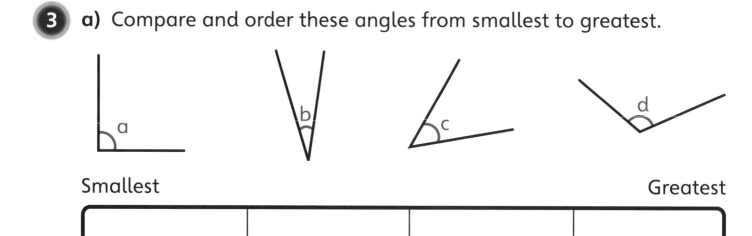

Smallest   Greatest

b) Compare and order these angles from greatest to smallest.

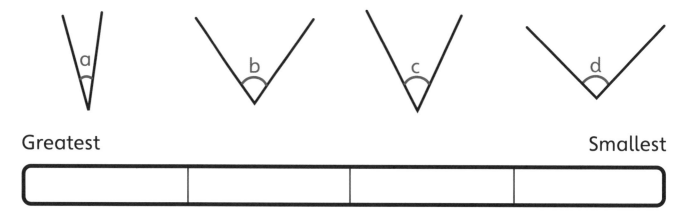

Greatest   Smallest

4 Finish drawing these angles so they are in ascending order of size.

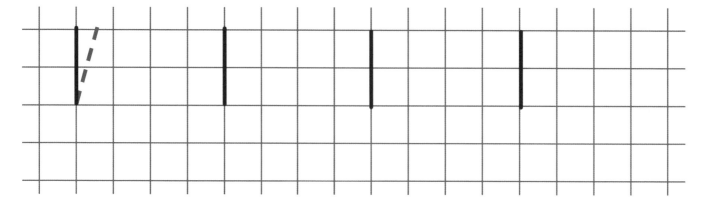

Can you include all three types of angle?

5 **a)** Compare and order these shapes in order of the size of their interior angle. Use a right-angle measurer to help.

CHALLENGE

A B C D

Smallest   Greatest

b) Do you notice a pattern between the type of shape and the size of the angles? Explain what you have noticed.

_____

_____

_____

_____

Reflect

How can you use what you know about right angles to help you identify acute and obtuse angles?

_____

_____

_____

Date: _____

Triangles

1 **a)** Circle all the equilateral triangles.

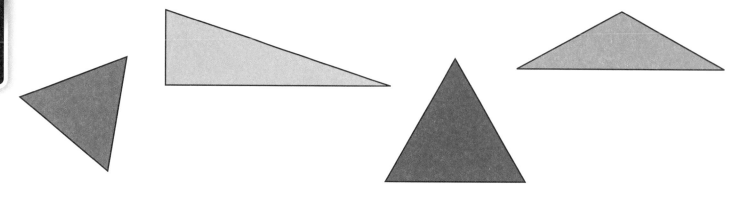

b) Circle all the isosceles triangles.

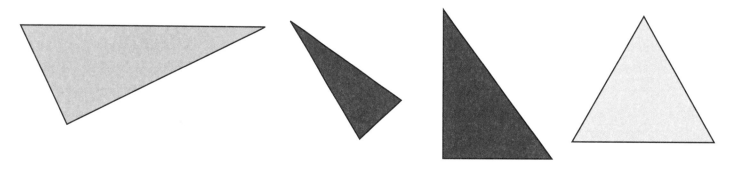

c) Circle all the scalene triangles.

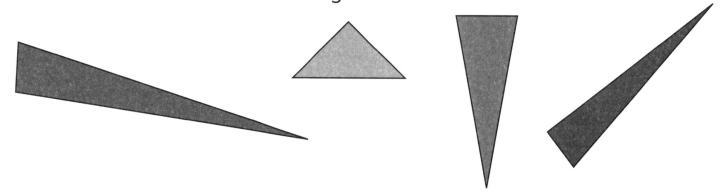

2 Shade this rug using different colours for the different types of triangle.

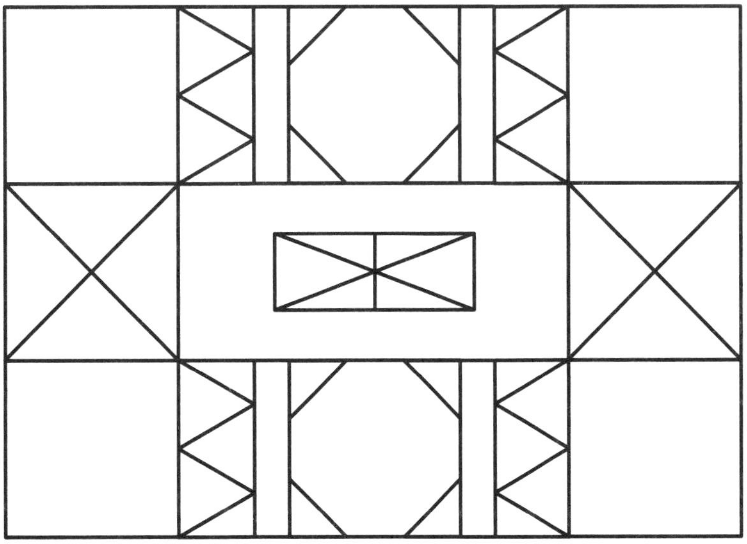

Key

Equilateral: ☐

Isosceles: ☐

Scalene: ☐

3 Draw two lines on the square to create an isosceles triangle and two right-angled triangles.

④ How many isosceles triangles can you find?

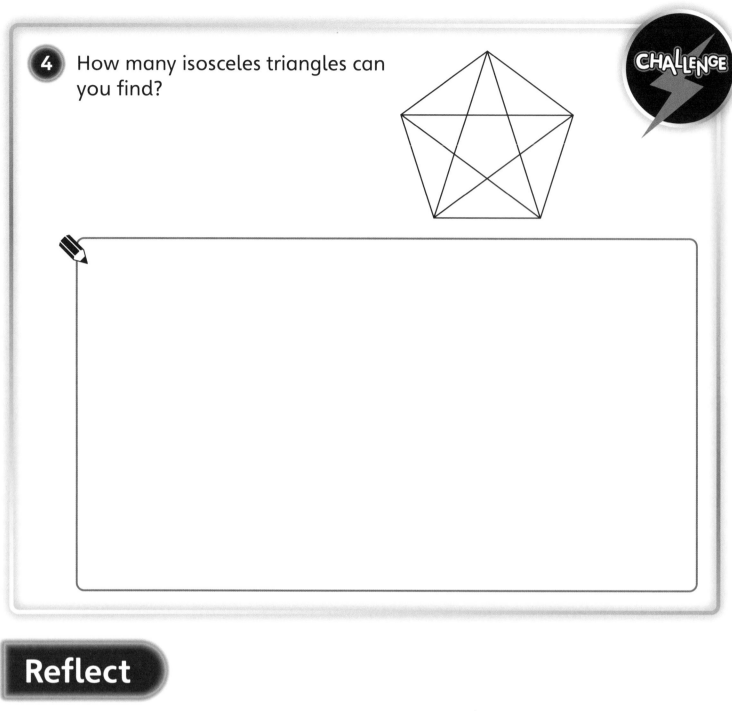

CHALLENGE

Reflect

Explain to a partner how each type of triangle is different to the others.

_____

_____

_____

Date: _____

Quadrilaterals

↓ Textbook 4C p104

1 **a)** Circle all the quadrilaterals.

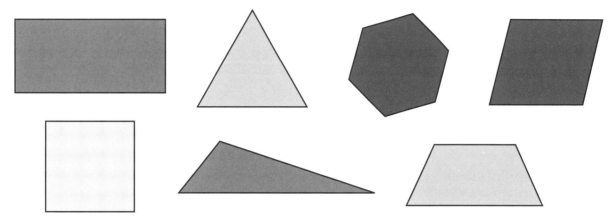

b) Circle all the **regular** quadrilaterals.

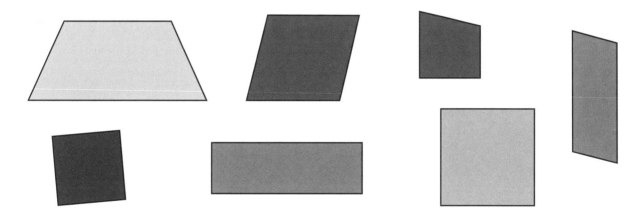

c) Circle all the **irregular** quadrilaterals.

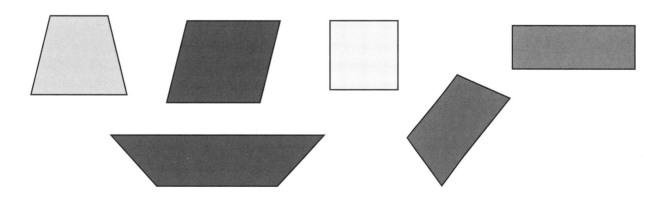

2 Draw two different regular and four different irregular quadrilaterals.

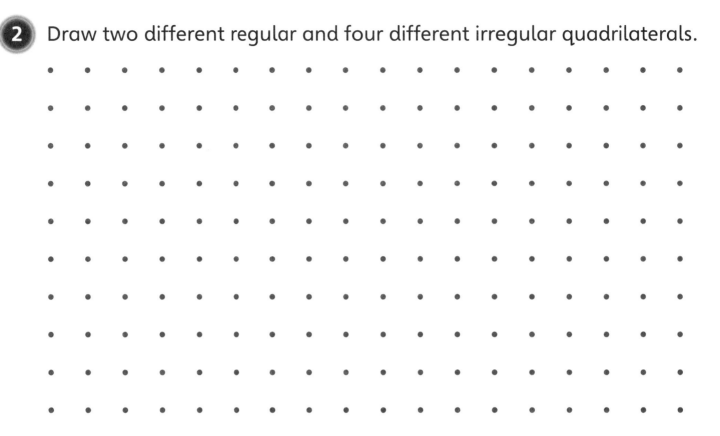

3 Match the names to the shapes.

Trapezium

Rhombus

Parallelogram

Rectangle

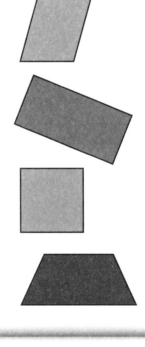

I wonder if I can call one of these a square too.

4 Draw two different quadrilaterals using the clues below:

- It is irregular.

- It has two acute angles.

- It has two angles greater than a right angle.

- It has two pairs of equal parallel sides.

Reflect

Explain why a square can always be identified as a rhombus but not all rhombuses are squares.

Date: _____

Polygons

1 **a)** Circle the **regular** polygons.

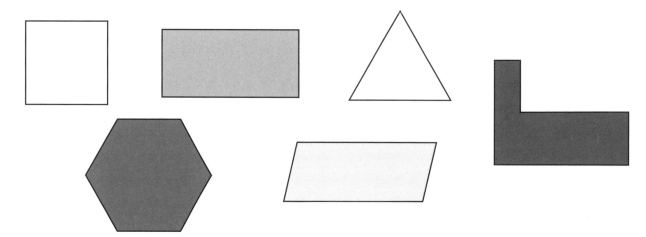

b) Circle the **irregular** polygons.

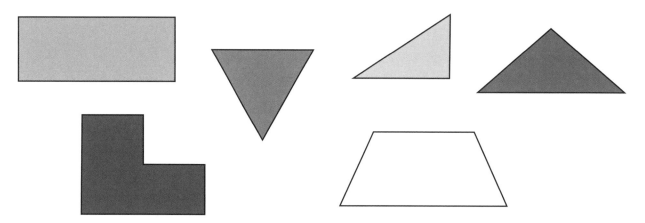

c) Shade the regular polygons in one colour and the irregular polygons in a different colour.

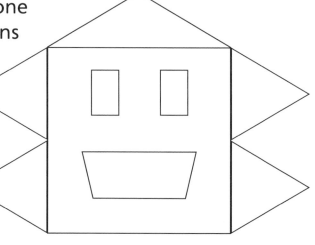

2 Draw two different regular 4-sided polygons.

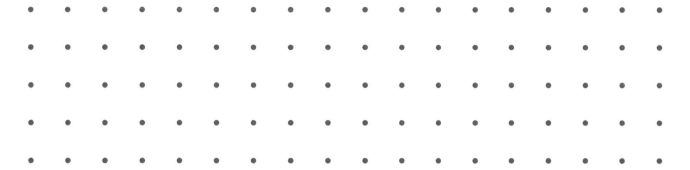

3 Draw a regular and an irregular 6-sided polygon.

4 Reena is describing a picture. Which one is she describing?

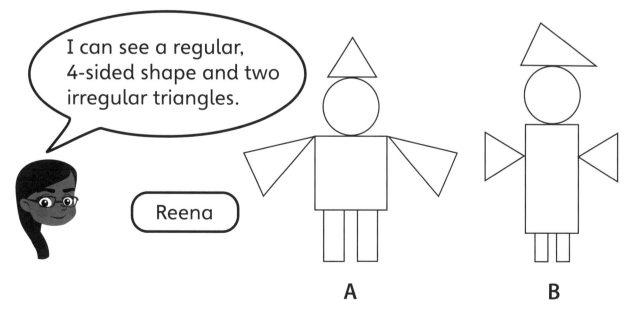

I can see a regular, 4-sided shape and two irregular triangles.

Reena

A   B

Reena is describing picture _____ .

5 Which of these shapes can be joined to create a regular hexagon? Circle the shapes that can be used. Draw two different solutions.

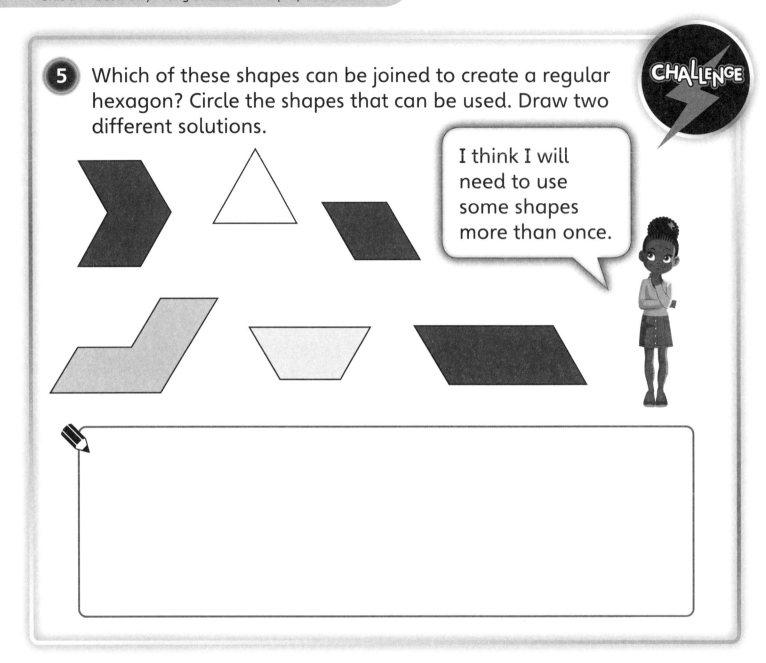

I think I will need to use some shapes more than once.

CHALLENGE

Reflect

Explain how you know whether or not a polygon is irregular.

_____

_____

_____

80

Date: _____

Reason about polygons

 a) Shade the shapes used to make the shaded shape on the left.

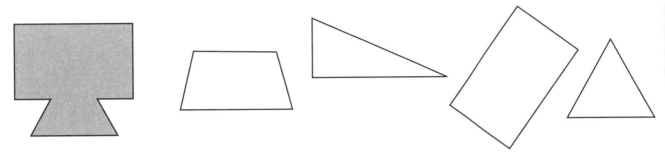

b) Shade the shapes used to make the shaded shape on the left.

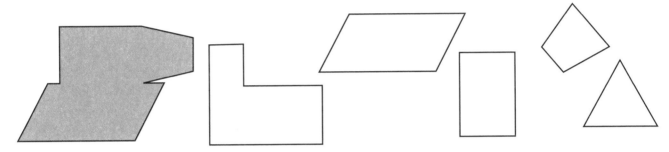

c) Shade the shapes used to make the shaded shape on the left.

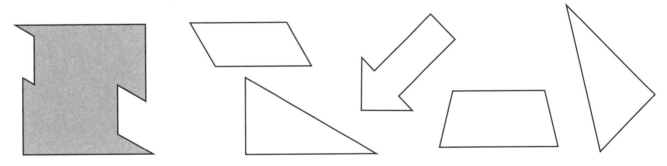

d) Shade the shapes used to make the shaded shape on the left.

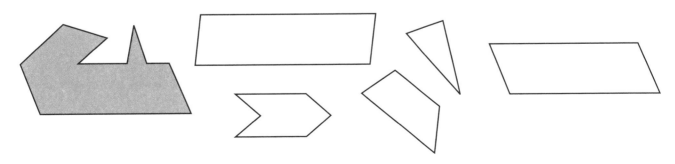

2 What shapes can be made by joining two triangles?

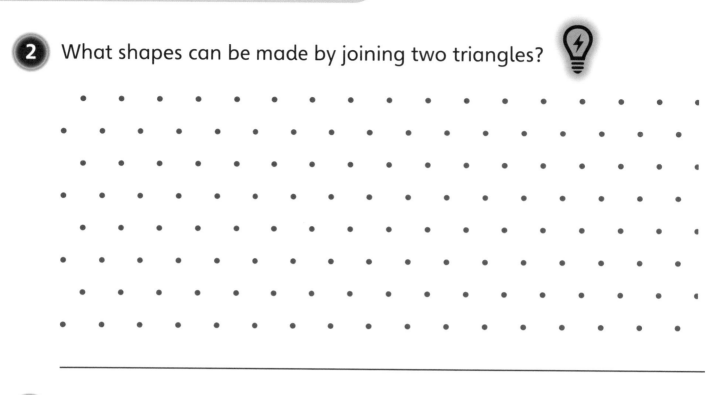

3 Part of this quadrilateral is hidden. What types of quadrilateral can this be? Draw and label the different types of quadrilateral it could be.

4 Complete the headings for the table below.

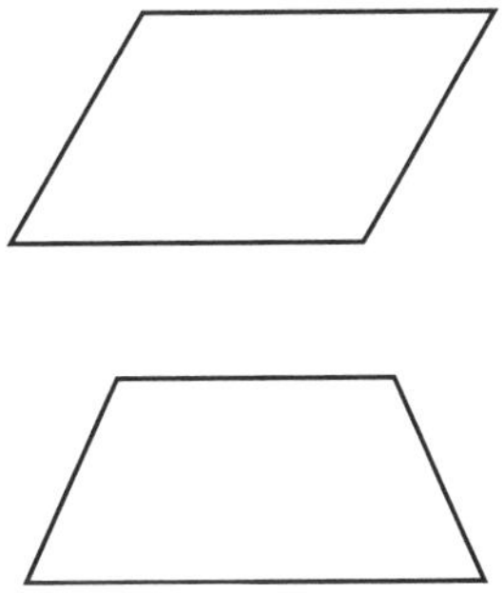

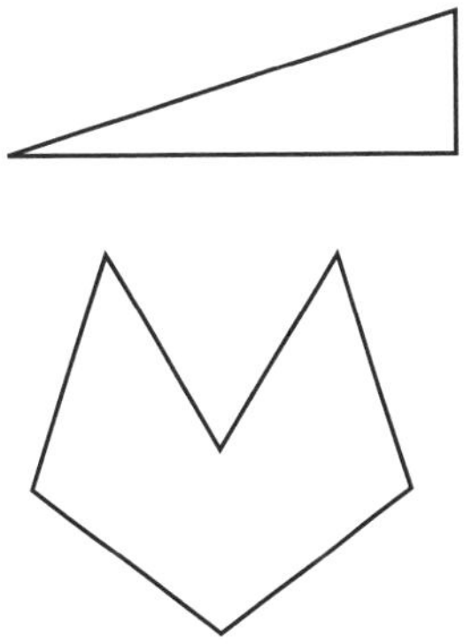

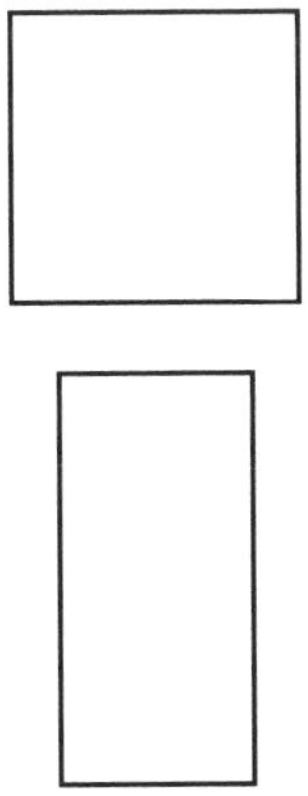

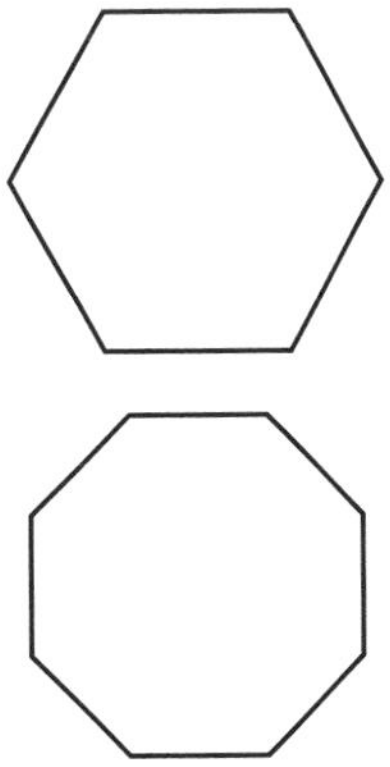

CHALLENGE

Reflect

To know what type of polygon I am looking at, I need to consider ___

_____

_____

_____.

Date: _____

Lines of symmetry

1 Find and draw the lines of symmetry in these flags.

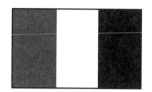  

2 Find and draw all the lines of symmetry in these polygons.

a) Isosceles triangle

c) Regular octagon

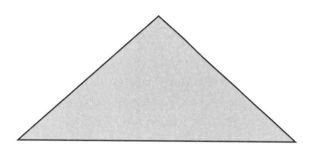 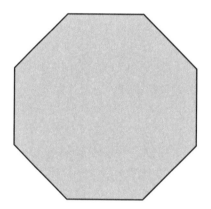

b) Rectangle

d) Irregular octagon

 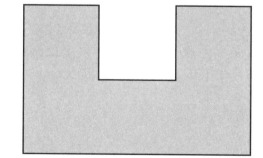

Textbook 4C p116

3 Draw the shapes in the table.

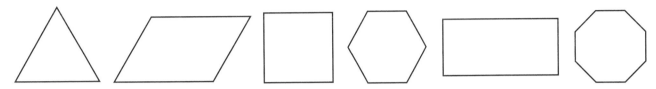

	Regular	Irregular
4 or more lines of symmetry		
Fewer than 4 lines of symmetry		

4 Draw an irregular hexagon that has two lines of symmetry.

85

5 Draw three different polygons:

CHALLENGE

a) A shape with exactly one line of symmetry.

b) A shape with exactly two lines of symmetry.

c) A shape with exactly three lines of symmetry.

Reflect

How many lines of symmetry are there in a circle? Explain your thinking to a partner.

Complete a symmetric figure

Textbook 4C p120

1 Complete the symmetric shapes. Name each shape once you have drawn it.

a)

Name of shape: _____

b)

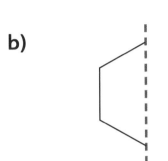

Name of shape: _____

c)

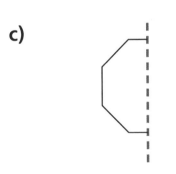

Name of shape: _____

d)

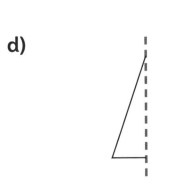

Name of shape: _____

2 Complete these symmetric patterns.

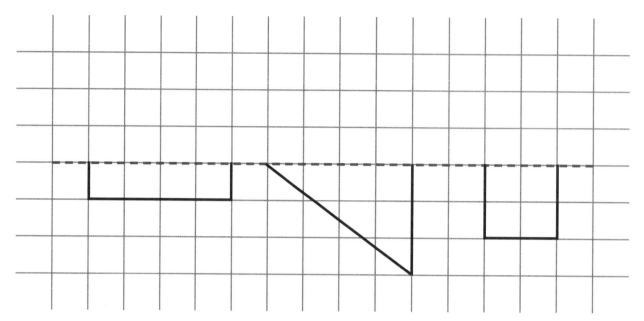

3 Complete the shape.

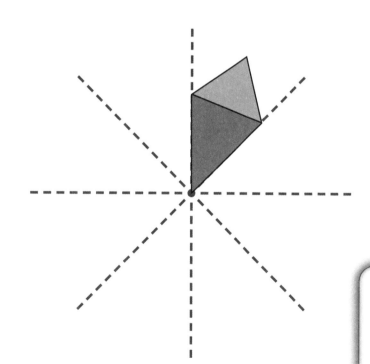

I will have to look closely to make sure I reflect the shapes in all the lines of symmetry.

4 Complete the shape. The two dotted lines are lines of symmetry.

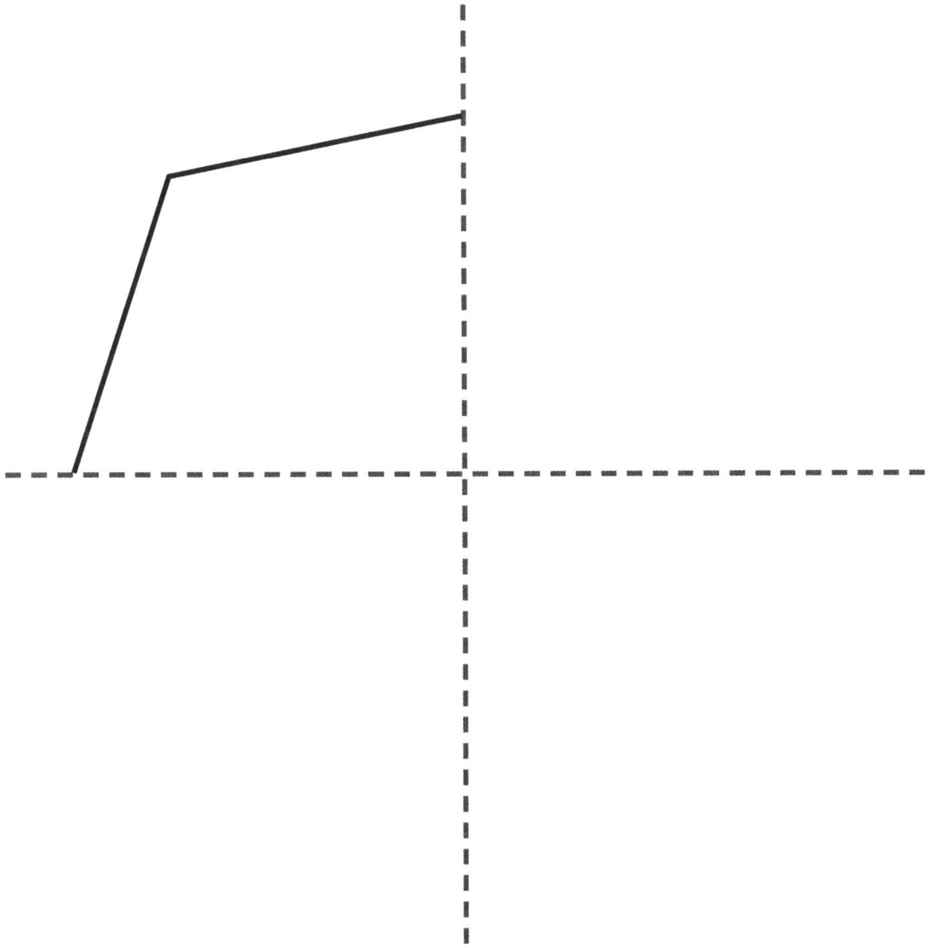

CHALLENGE

Reflect

When completing a symmetric shape, it is important to _____

_____

_____

_____ .

Date: _____

End of unit check

My journal

↑ Textbook 4C p124

I Draw **two** straight lines across the hexagon to make two triangles and two quadrilaterals.

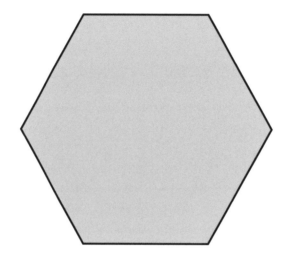

How many solutions can you find?

2 Greg draws a triangle. He says, 'Two of the three angles in my triangle are obtuse.'

Prove why Greg **cannot** be correct.

_____

_____

_____

_____

_____

Power check

How do you feel about your work in this unit?

Power puzzle

Is it possible to fold an A4 piece of paper to make a square?

How about an isosceles triangle or an equilateral triangle?

Show a partner. Can they work out how you did it?

Date: _____

Interpret charts

↓ Textbook 4C p128

1 Kieron and Amy collect 'Ninja Woman' collecting cards.

Kieron's Ninja Woman cards

	Number
shiny	
normal	
limited edition	
jigsaw piece	

Each ☐ represents 8 cards.

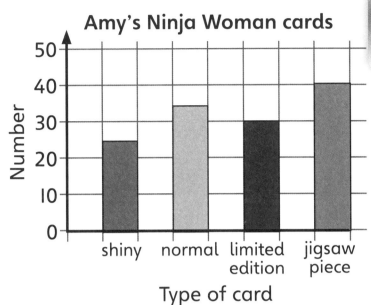

Amy's Ninja Woman cards

a) How many jigsaw piece cards does Kieron have?

b) How many normal cards does Kieron have?

c) How many shiny cards does Amy have?

93

2 Use the data from the table to complete these sentences.

Number of books read during Year 4

	Evie	Gracie
Non-fiction	7	8
Fiction	22	23
Poetry	3	6
Total	32	37

Evie read ☐ fiction books.

Gracie read ☐ non-fiction books.

Gracie read ☐ books in total.

3 Use the information in the table in Question 2 to create a pictogram for the number of non-fiction books read.

Number of non-fiction books read

	Number of books
Evie	
Gracie	

Each ■ represents 2 books.

4 Complete the missing information.

Number of pages read in one term

Milo	
Luis	4,500
Grace	
Finlay	2,250

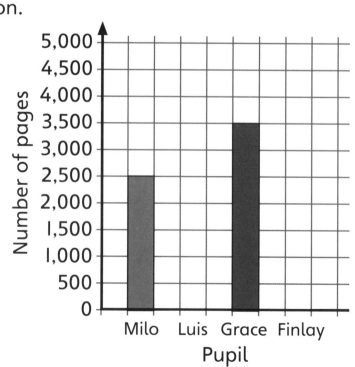

5 Complete the pictogram and bar chart using the data in the table.

 CHALLENGE

Number of class points earnt last term

	Year 3	Year 4	Year 5	Year 6
Earth	275	225	300	200
Air	350	400	225	375
Fire	325	375	300	350
Water	450	450	300	350

Number of class points per team in Year 4

	Number of points
Earth	
Air	
Fire	
Water	●●●●◖

Each ● represents ☐ points.

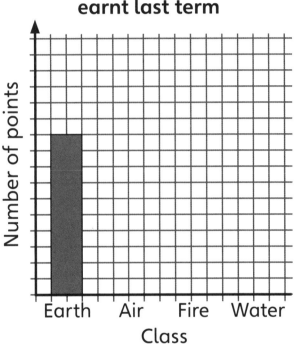

Total number of class points earnt last term

Reflect

Which is the best way to display data? Discuss with a partner and write your answer.

Date: _____

Solve problems with charts

1 The pictogram and bar chart show the number of marbles won in a contest in December and May.

Number of marbles won in December

	Number of marbles
Tom	◠ ◠
Alice	◠ ◠ ◠ (
Zac	◠ ◠ (
Ambika	◠ (

Each ◠ represents 6 marbles.

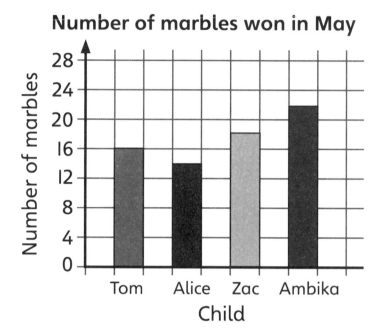

a) How many marbles did Alice win in December and May altogether?

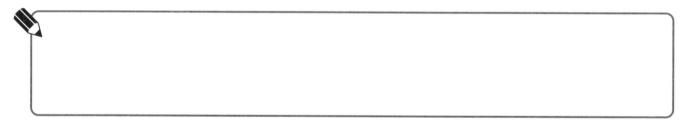

b) How many more marbles did Zac win in May compared to Alice?

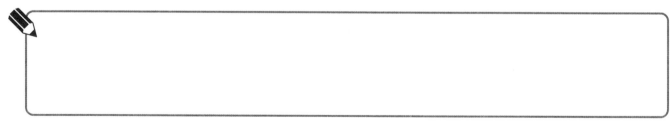

c) How many marbles did the children win in May altogether?

2 This table shows the number of visitors to the History Museum and the Science Museum over 3 days.

Complete the table.

Number of visitors

	History Museum	Science Museum	Total
Saturday	625		1,425
Sunday	745	725	
Monday		390	780

3 Sarah and Max are playing video games. Use the information below to complete the table, then complete a bar chart showing the scores for Sarah.

Sarah scored 450 more on Vault Explorer than Max.

Max scored 250 more on Climbing Road than he did on Space Raiders.

Number of points earned

	Space Raiders	Vault Explorer	Climbing Road
Sarah	700		850
Max	550	200	

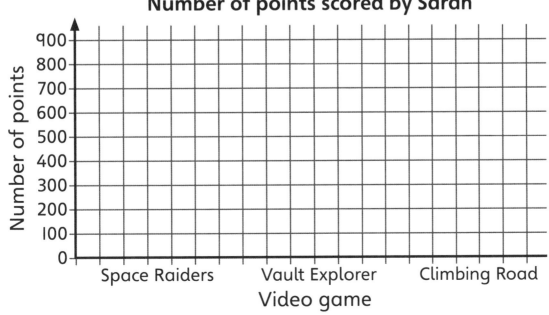

Number of points scored by Sarah

(y-axis: Number of points, 0–900; x-axis: Video game — Space Raiders, Vault Explorer, Climbing Road)

97

4 The bar chart shows the number of children who have a packed lunch and a hot lunch each day.

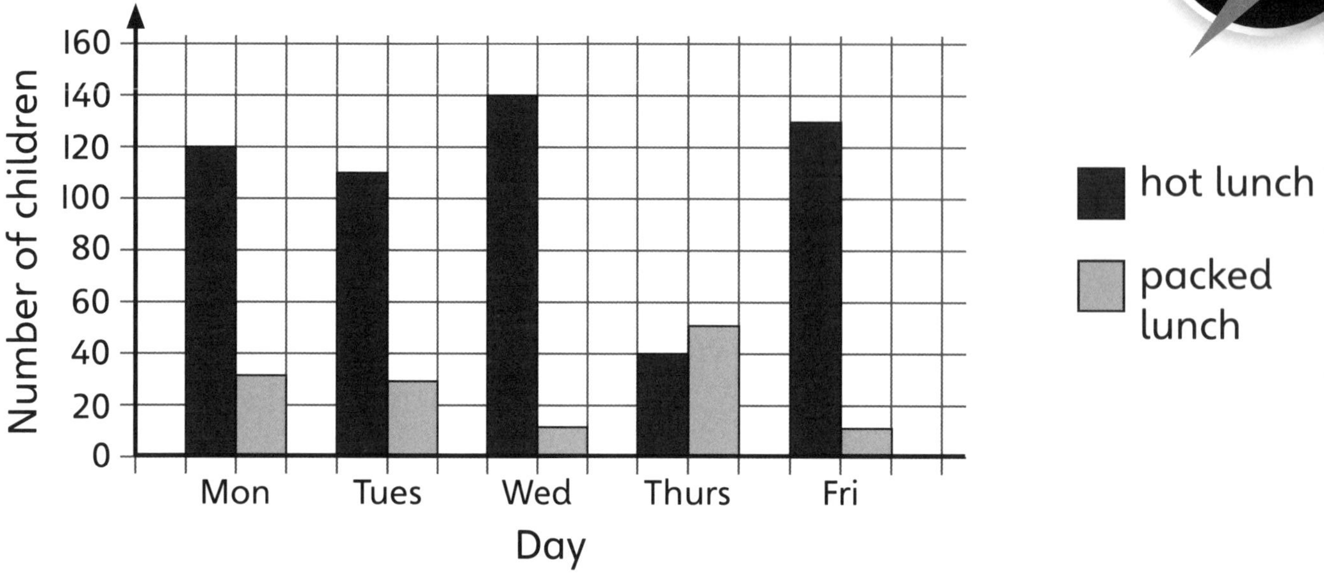

CHALLENGE

hot lunch

packed lunch

a) There are 160 children in the school.

Each child has to have a packed lunch or a hot lunch.

How many children were off school on Friday? ☐

b) Which day was there the greatest difference between the

number of children who had a hot lunch and those that had a

packed lunch? _____ . What was the difference? ☐

Reflect

What types of graph do you know? Which do you prefer? Why?

● _____

● _____

● _____

●

Solve problems with charts ❷

→ Textbook 4C p136

1 Some children counted the number of steps they took in one day. Their results are shown in the bar chart.

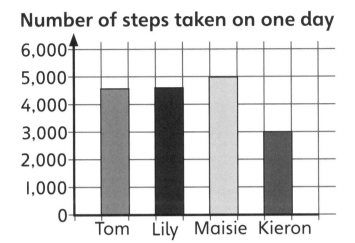

Number of steps taken on one day

a) How many more steps did Lily and Maisie take compared to Tom and Kieron?

b) Gracie walked 1,500 more steps than Maisie. How many steps did Gracie walk?

2

Temperatures in June

	Highest temperature	Lowest temperature
London	28 °C	12 °C
Cardiff	19 °C	12 °C
Belfast	30 °C	15 °C
Edinburgh	23 °C	12 °C

a) What is the difference between the highest and lowest temperature in Cardiff?   ☐ °C

b) Which city's highest temperature is double its lowest temperature?   _____

c) Which city has the largest difference between its highest and lowest temperature?   _____

99

3 Otis went on a sponsored walk over 5 days.

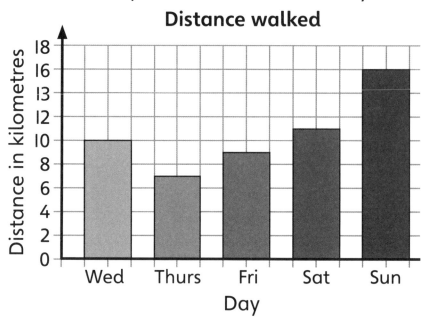

a) How far did Otis walk in total?

b) How much further did Otis walk on Sunday than Saturday?

c) Otis was sponsored £6 per kilometre. How much did Otis raise on Wednesday?

4 Estimate the difference between the populations of Glastonbury and Overton.

Population of different towns

	Population
Windermere	● ● ◖
Twyford	● ● ● ◕
Glastonbury	● ● ● ● ◢
Battle	● ● ●

Each ● represents 2,000 people.

Population of different towns

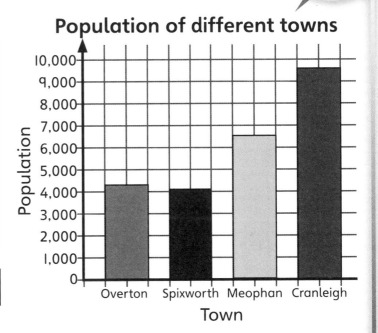

Reflect

Look at the pictogram and bar chart in question 4.

Write two questions for a partner to answer based on these representations.

Date: _____

Interpret line graphs

1. This line graph shows Holly's car journey to visit her family.

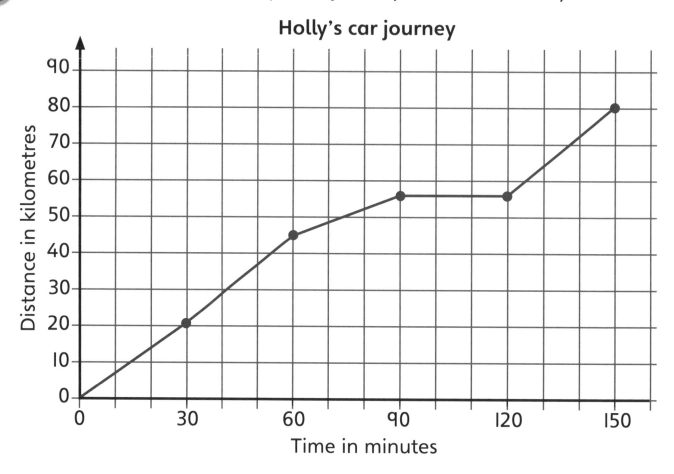

Holly's car journey

a) How many kilometres had Holly travelled after 30 minutes?

[ ] km

b) How many kilometres had she travelled after 90 minutes?

[ ] km

c) How long did it take Holly to travel 45 km?

[ ] minutes

d) How long did the journey take from start to finish?

[ ] minutes

2 The line graph shows the length of the shadow cast by a stick over one day.

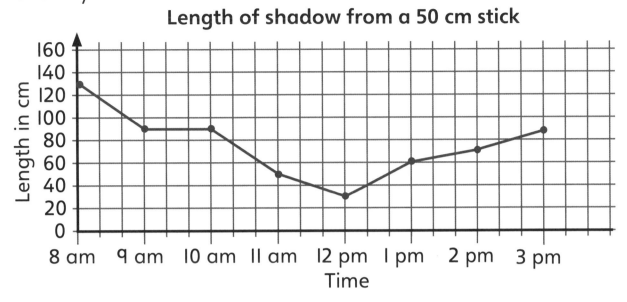

Length of shadow from a 50 cm stick

a) What was the length of the shadow at 8:30 am?

☐ cm

b) When was the shadow 30 cm? _____

c) Complete the sentences.

The shadow was the longest at _____ . It was ☐ cm long.

The shadow was the shortest at _____ . It was ☐ cm long.

The shadow was the same length at both _____ and _____ .

3 Would a line graph be a good way to present this data? Explain your reasoning.

_____

_____

_____

_____

People's favourite colour

Blue	12
Yellow	10
Green	16
Red	8

4

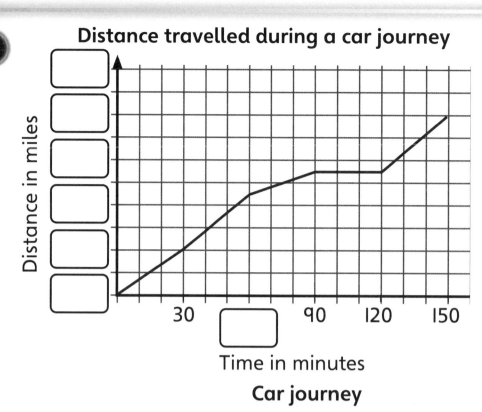

Distance travelled during a car journey

CHALLENGE

Distance in miles

Time in minutes

Car journey

Time	30 minutes		90 minutes	120 minutes	150 minutes
Distance		45 miles			

a) Complete the table and the axes on the line graph.

b) When was the car stuck in a traffic jam? Explain your answer.

_____

_____

Reflect

When would you use a line graph instead of a bar chart?

• _____

• _____

•

Date: _____

Interpret line graphs ❷

An open container was put out in the rain. The amount of rainwater it collected is shown in the line graph.

Textbook 4C p144

a) How much more rainwater was in the container at II am than at 10 am?

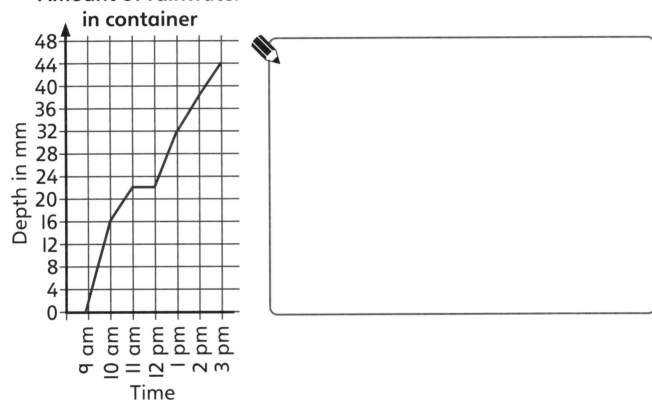

Amount of rainwater in container

b) Complete the sentence.

It took ⬜ hours for the water level to increase from 22 mm to 32 mm.

Explain why it took this long. How do you know?

_____

_____

_____

_____

2 **a)** How many steps did Evie take during the day?

[ ]

b) How many steps did Evie take between 12 pm and 3 pm?

c) How long did Evie take to go from 500 to 1,500 steps?

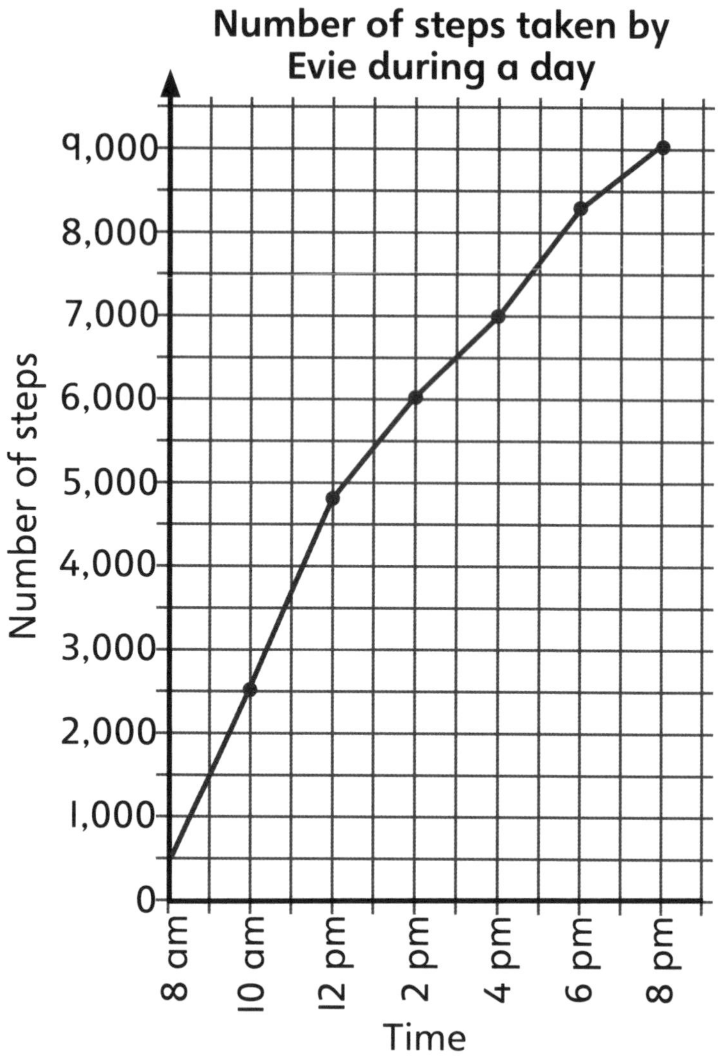

Number of steps taken by Evie during a day

3 Lee hits a golf ball.

The graph shows the height of the ball off the ground at different times.

What is the greatest height the ball reaches?

[ ]

How do you know?

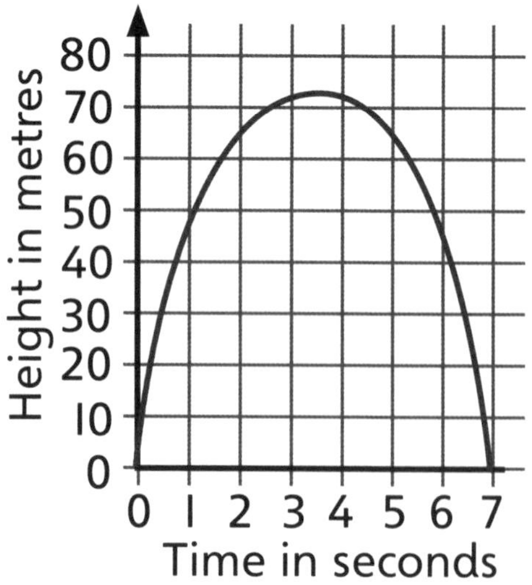

4 This line graph shows the temperature in Spain in July and December. Write five statements about this line graph. Use the words below to help you.

CHALLENGE

warmer, colder, difference, same, different, more than, less than

_____

_____

_____

_____

_____

_____

_____

_____

_____

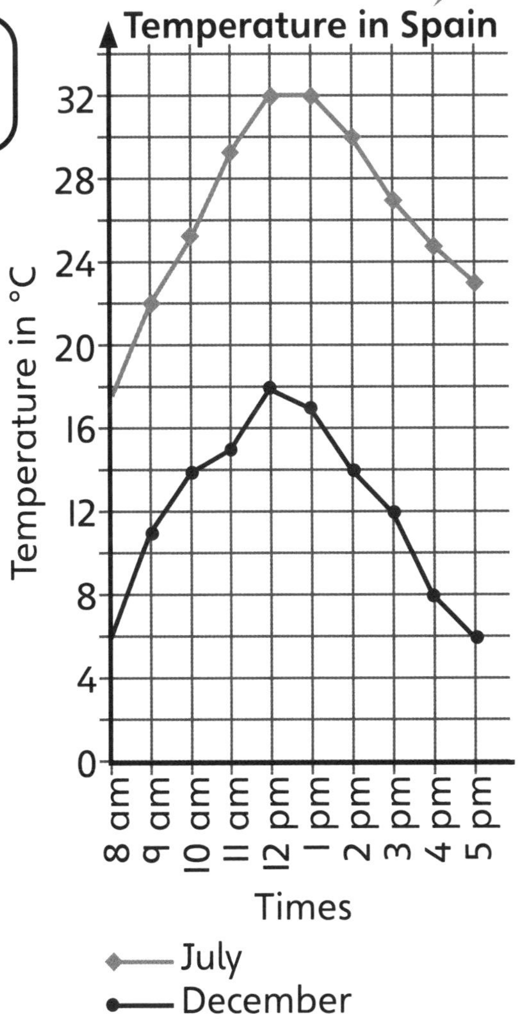

Temperature in Spain

Temperature in °C

32
28
24
20
16
12
8
4
0

8 am, 9 am, 10 am, 11 am, 12 pm, 1 pm, 2 pm, 3 pm, 4 pm, 5 pm

Times

◆—— July
●—— December

Reflect

Write some reflections on this lesson.

One important thing I am going to remember when looking at line graph data is _____

_____.

Date: _____

Draw line graphs

1 Ebo is running a race.

The table shows his progress.

	Distance from start	Time at checkpoint
Checkpoint A	5 km	30 minutes
Checkpoint B	8 km	50 minutes
Checkpoint C	10 km	75 minutes
Finish	12 km	90 minutes

Represent this information on a line graph.

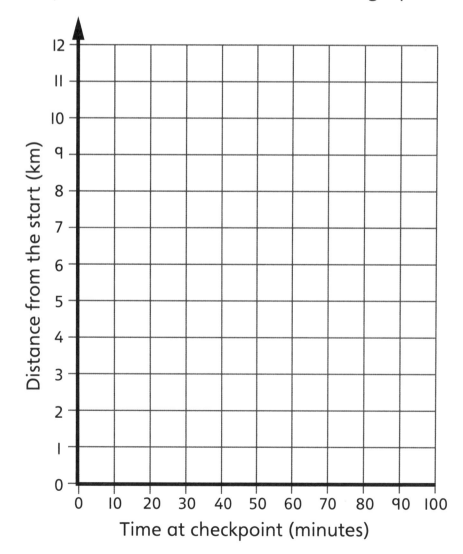

Distance from the start (km)

Time at checkpoint (minutes)

2 Holly buys a new car for £25,000.
The table shows how much the car is worth over the next 8 years.

End of year	1	2	3	4	5	6	7	8
Value	£20,000	£16,000	£14,000	£10,500	£8,000	£4,000	£3,000	£2,500

a) Represent this information on a line graph.

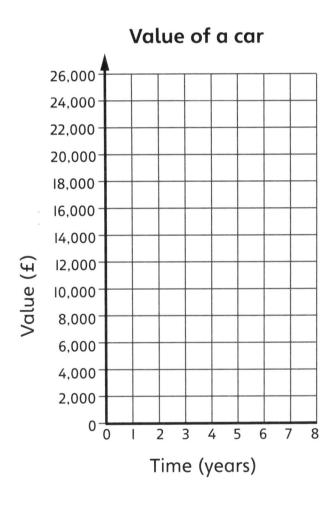

Value of a car

b) In which two years does the car lose the most value?

_____

Discuss with a partner how you can tell by looking at the line graph.

3 Here is a table showing the orders in a cafe one afternoon.

CHALLENGE

Item	Coffee	Tea	Sandwich	Cake
Number	22	15	11	16

a) Explain why you cannot represent this data on a line graph.

_____

_____

b) What type of data would you represent with a line graph? Give some examples.

_____

_____

c) Why do we sometimes use a dotted line on a line graph rather than a solid line?

_____

_____

Reflect

Discuss with a partner about what is the same and what is different about a line graph and a bar graph.

End of unit check

Textbook 4C p152

My journal

This line graph shows the price of Tom's toy car that he is selling in an auction.

Write three bits of information you can tell from the line graph. Use some of the words below to help you.

Keywords: more than, altogether, total, less than, compared to

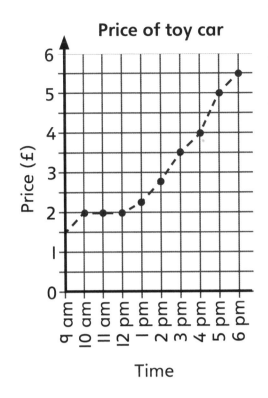

Price of toy car

_____

_____

_____

_____

_____

_____

Power check

How do you feel about your work in this unit?

Power puzzle

1 Jamie measured the height of four children in her class.
She created bar charts to represent the data.

Use the bar charts and the clues below to help you complete
the missing information.

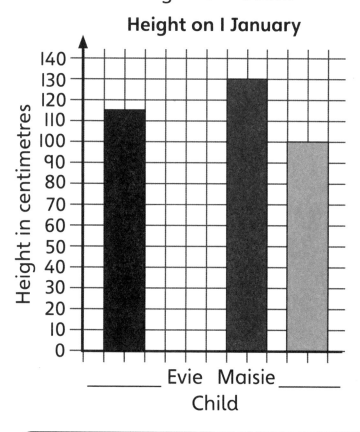

Height on 1 January

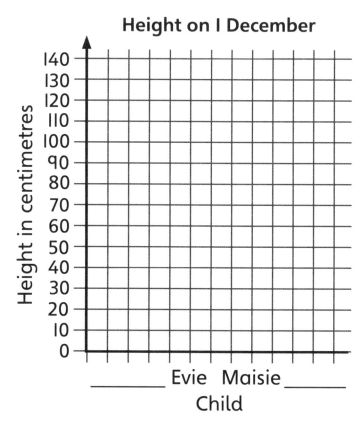

Height on 1 December

Maisie was 130 cm tall in January
and grew 5 cm between January
and December.

Raj was 15 cm shorter than the next
shortest child in January.

Finlay was 15 cm shorter than
Maisie in January, but only 10 cm
shorter than Maisie in December.

In December, Maisie was the
same height as Evie.

Evie grew 15 cm between
January and December.

Raj was 10 cm shorter than
Finlay in December.

2 Measure your height and the height of three other children in your class. Draw a pictogram and bar chart to represent the data.

Date: _____

Describe position

1 Use the map to identify places from the information given.

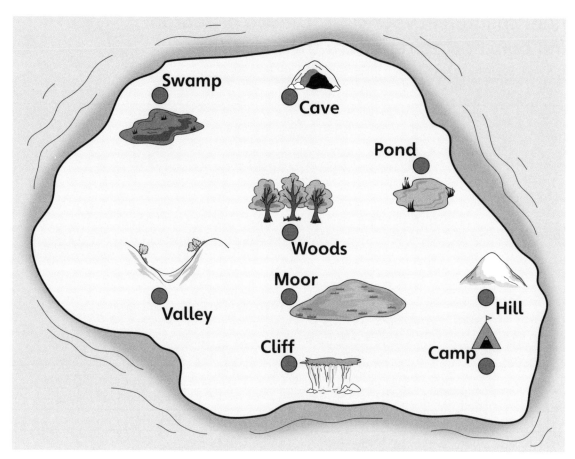

a) This place is next to the moor and close to the camp.

_____

b) This place is in the centre of the map.

_____

c) This place is between the cliff and the cave. It is closer to the cliff than the cave.

_____

d) This is the closest place to the camp.

_____

2 Using the map from question I, describe where these places are.

a) The camp _____

_____

b) The cave _____

_____

c) The pond _____

_____

d) The swamp _____

_____

e) The moor _____

_____

f) The cliff _____

_____

3 Imagine drawing a straight line from the valley to the pond, on the map in question I.

Which other places would the line go through?

_____

4

Andy

The woods are exactly half-way between the cave and the moor.

Is Andy correct? Explain your answer.

_____

_____

5 Here is another version of the map.

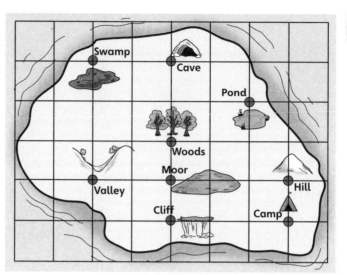

a) Use this version of the map to describe where some places are. Ask a partner to find them.

_____

_____

b) Does this version make it more efficient to say where the places are? Explain your answer.

_____

_____

Reflect

How can maps and grids help you to explain where things are?

_____

_____

_____

Describe position using coordinates

↓ Textbook 4C p160

1 Jamie made a sketch of her garden.

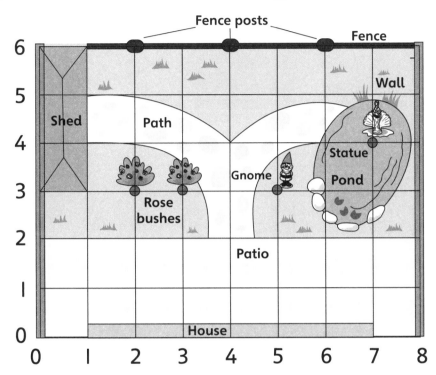

a) What are the coordinates of the statue?

The statue is at (☐ , ☐).

b) There is a fence post at (2,6). Where are the other fence posts?

The other fence posts are at (☐ , ☐) and (☐ , ☐).

c) One of the rose bushes is at (2,3). Where is the other one?

The other rose bush is at (☐ , ☐).

2 The coordinates of one corner of the shed are (1,3).

What are the coordinates of the other three corners?

(☐ , ☐), (☐ , ☐) and (☐ , ☐).

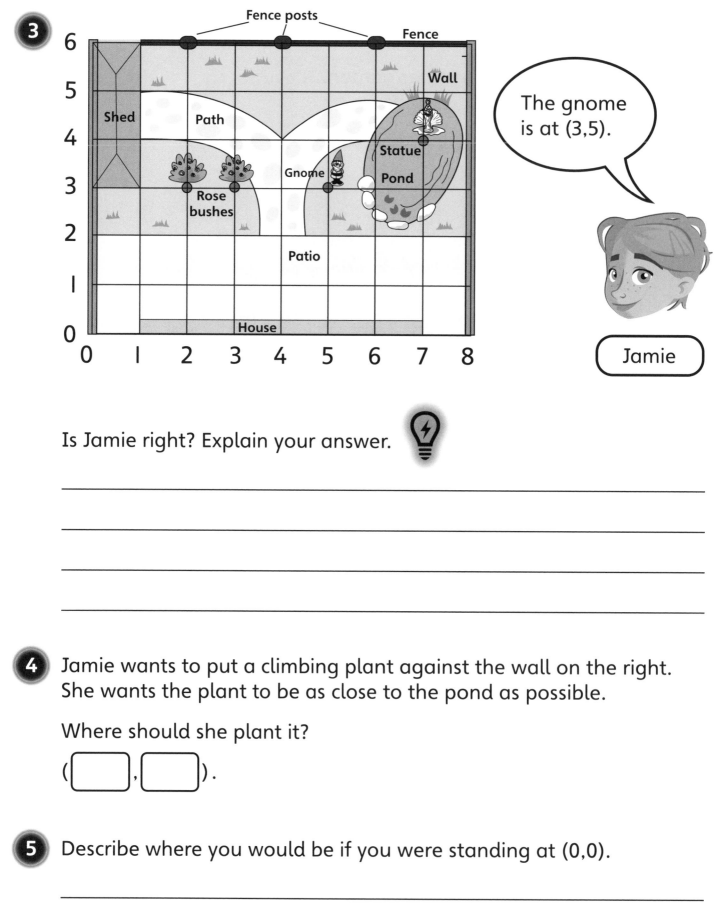

3

The gnome is at (3,5).

Jamie

Is Jamie right? Explain your answer.

_____

_____

_____

_____

4 Jamie wants to put a climbing plant against the wall on the right. She wants the plant to be as close to the pond as possible.

Where should she plant it?

(⬚ , ⬚).

5 Describe where you would be if you were standing at (0,0).

_____

6 There is a spade in the shed. What could its position be if it is:

a) As far away from the house as possible? (☐ , ☐)

b) As close to the house as possible? (☐ , ☐)

7 Which one of these positions would be a good place to plant a bush? Explain your answer.

CHALLENGE

A (1,4) B (4,1) C (4,3) D (4,5) E (7,3)

(☐ , ☐)

I think this because _____

_____

_____

_____

(2,4) means start at (0,0) and go
2 squares up and then 4 squares right.

Reflect

Do you agree with Ebo? Explain your answer.   Ebo

_____

_____

_____

Date: _____

Plot coordinates

1 For each grid, plot the points and draw a straight line through them.

a) (3,1), (4,1), (7,1), (8,1)

b) (2,2), (4,4), (6,6), (7,7)

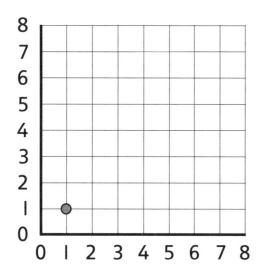 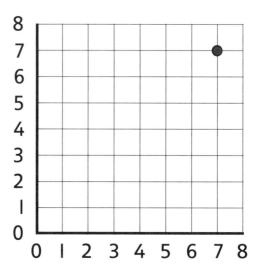

2 Draw these straight-sided shapes on the grids. What shapes are they?

a) Vertices at (1,5), (1,7) and (4,6).

b) Vertices at (1,1), (3,1), (3,4), (2,4) and (1,3).

_____ _____

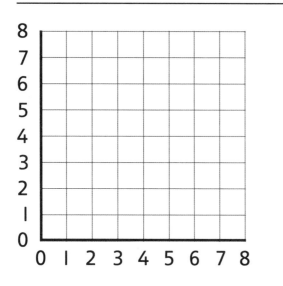 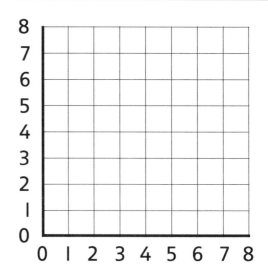

3 Plot the following points to make a line.

a) (0,3)

(1,3)

(2,3)

(3,3)

(4,3)

(5,3)

(6,3)

(7,3)

(8,3)

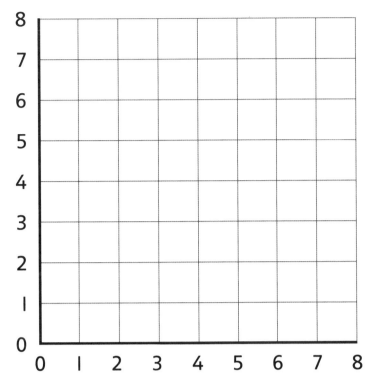

b) (5,8)

(5,7)

(5,6)

(5,5)

(5,4)

(5,3)

(5,2)

(5,1)

(5,0)

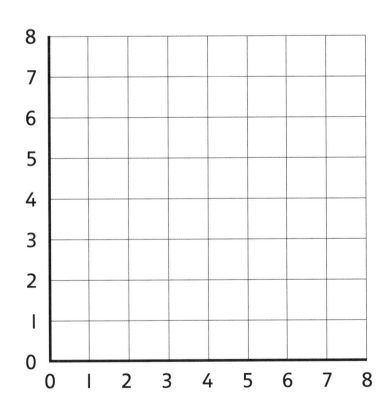

4 **a)** Draw a design for a star shape on this grid.

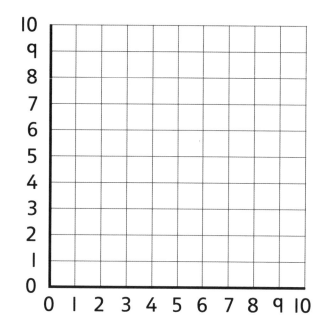

b) Write the coordinates of all the vertices.

_____

_____

_____

Reflect

(3,9) and (3,5) are two points on the same straight line.
Is the line horizontal or vertical? Explain your answer.

_____

_____

_____

Draw 2D shapes on a grid

1 Amelia is drawing a rectangle.

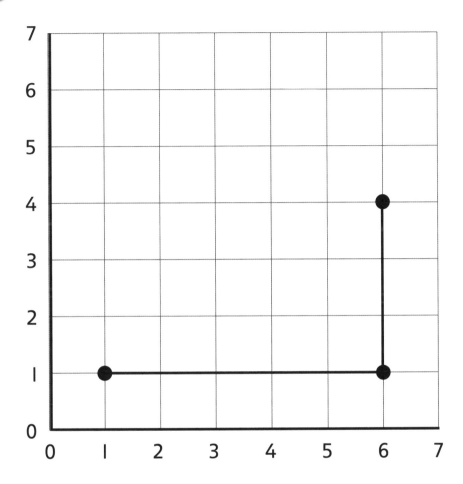

Complete the rectangle and write the coordinates of all four vertices.

 .

 .

(⬚ , ⬚) .

(⬚ , ⬚) .

2 Mo is drawing a square on the grid with sides 4 units in length. He has already plotted a point for the bottom left corner of the square.

a) Work out the coordinates of the other corners.

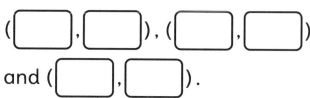

b) Draw the square.

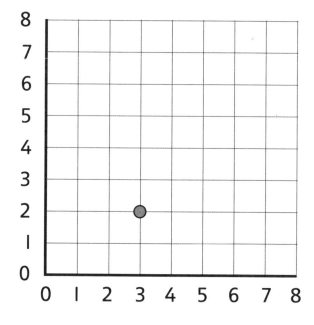

3 Carrie draws another rectangle exactly the same size as this one. Write down a possible set of coordinates for the other rectangle.

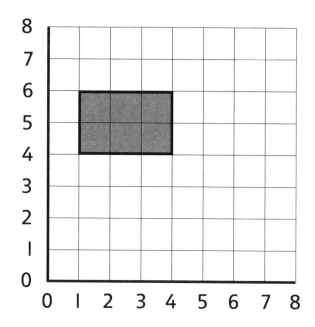

4 This is part of a shape.

(2,3)

0

CHALLENGE

a) What are the coordinates of the other vertices if the shape is a square with sides of 6 units?

([   ] , [   ]) , ([   ] , [   ]) and ([   ] , [   ]) .

b) What are the coordinates of the other vertices if the shape is a rectangle with sides of 5 and 7 units? (There is more than one answer.)

Answer 1: ([   ] , [   ]) , ([   ] , [   ]) and ([   ] , [   ]) .

Answer 2: ([   ] , [   ]) , ([   ] , [   ]) and ([   ] , [   ]) .

Reflect

Apart from coordinates, what other mathematical knowledge did you use in this lesson? How did you use this knowledge to answer questions on coordinates?

- _____
- _____
- _____

Date: _____

Translate on a grid

1 On this chart, the instruction 1 right, 1 down will move the boat to the island.

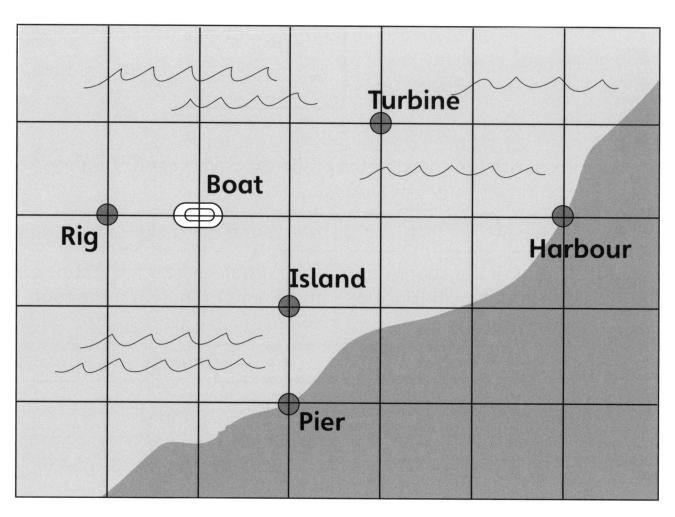

Where would these instructions take the boat? Start back at the same place each time.

a) 1 right, 2 down _____

b) 2 right, 1 up _____

c) 1 left _____

d) 4 right _____

2 A robot starts at (5,5) and makes these moves from point to point around the grid:

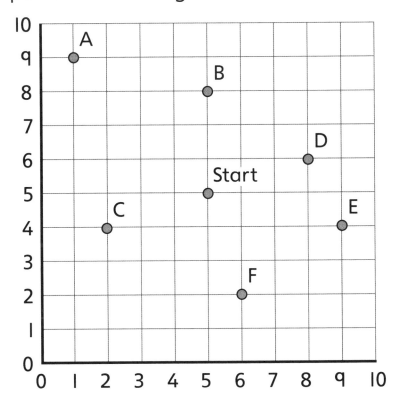

3 right, 1 up

7 left, 3 up

1 right, 5 down

3 right, 4 up

1 right, 6 down

3 right, 2 up

In what order does the robot visit the points?

Start → D → _____ → _____ → _____ → _____ → _____

3 Starting at (2,2), the instruction 2 right, 1 up takes you to (4,3).

Always starting from (2,2), where would these instructions take you?

a) 2 right, 1 down   (⬚ , ⬚)

b) 1 left, 1 up   (⬚ , ⬚)

c) 2 left, 2 down   (⬚ , ⬚)

d) 0 right, 2 up   (⬚ , ⬚)

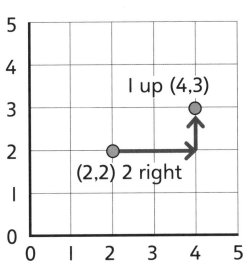

4 **a)** You start at the point (100,100). Where would the translation

26 left, 26 up take you? (⬚ , ⬚)

b) You make the translation (28 right, 28 down) and arrive

at (100,100). Where did you start? (⬚ , ⬚)

5 The rectangle is translated 6 right and 5 up. What are the coordinates of the vertices of the rectangle in its new position?

CHALLENGE

(⬚ , ⬚)

(⬚ , ⬚)

(⬚ , ⬚)

(⬚ , ⬚)

Reflect

The coordinates at the start and end of a translation can tell you whether you moved up or down, and left or right.

Do you agree? Explain your answer.

_____

_____

_____

Describe translation on a grid

1 This map shows the rows of bookshelves in a library.

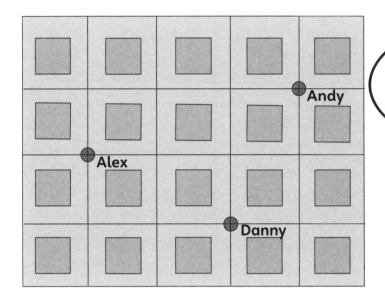

I am going to meet Danny. I will count shelves; I need to go 2 right and 1 down.

Alex

Describe these journeys.

a) Andy goes to meet Danny.

Andy goes ☐ left, ☐ down

b) Danny goes to meet Alex.

Danny goes ☐ _____ , ☐ _____

c) Danny goes to meet Andy.

Andy goes _____ , _____

d) Andy goes to meet Alex.

Andy goes _____

2 To go from A to B, translate **I right, 3 up** or **3 up, I right**.

Describe these translations:

a) B to A

[ ] ——— , [ ] ———

b) B to C

[ ] ——— , [ ] ———

c) E to D

_____ , _____

d) D to E

_____ , _____

e) D to C

_____

f) A to D

_____

(Grid showing points: A at (1,3), B at (2,6), C at (7,7), D at (4,3), E at (6,1). Axes both labelled 0 to 8.)

3

First I moved 3 right and 2 up; then I moved I left and I up.

Reena

Describe Reena's complete journey.

Reena moved _____

4 This chess piece can move to any of the squares marked with a white circle.

How would you describe each of these moves?

_____

_____

CHALLENGE

_____

_____

_____

_____

_____

Reflect

You know the numbers that describe a translation (for example, 5 left, 2 up).

How would you describe the reverse translation that would take you back to your starting position?

_____

_____

_____

Date: _____

End of unit check

My journal

1 Start at (5,5). Choose two cards and make the translations shown on the cards, one after the other.

Example: Cards A and F will take you from (5,5) to (9,6).

| A | 5 left, 10 up |
| D | 10 right, 5 down |

| B | 9 left, 9 up |
| E | 14 left, 4 up |

| C | 2 left, 3 up |
| F | 9 right, 9 down |

Which pair of cards will take you from (5,5) to (10,10)? Explain your answer.

Cards _____ and _____ will take you from (5,5) to (10,10) because ____

_____

_____

_____

2 Jamir and Kim are playing a game of 4-in-a-line.

- The first player to get four of their counters in any straight line wins the game.

- Jamir has just put a counter in position (5,3).

It is Kim's turn to place a black counter. What position should she put it in to win the game?

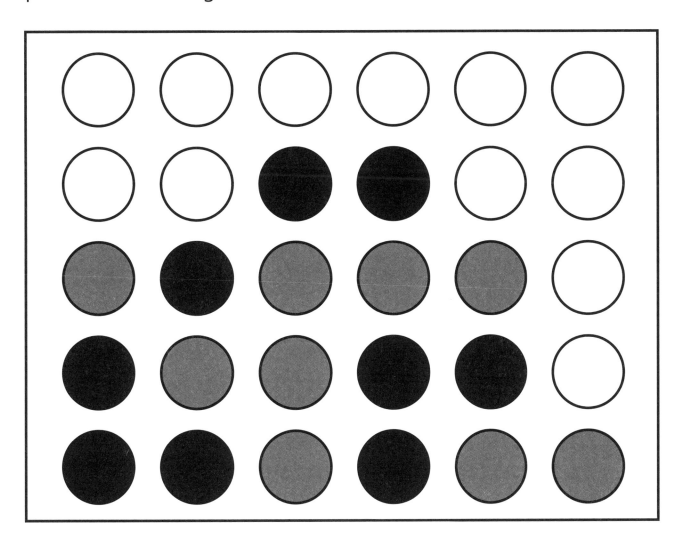

Power check

How do you feel about your work in this unit?

Power play

Coordinate battleships is a game for two players.

- Agree patterns of dots to represent ships with a partner.

- Mark your ships on your grid – do not let your partner see where you put them! Your ships must not touch each other.

- Take turns to pick coordinates. Tell your partner whether their shot was a hit or a miss.

- Sink all your partner's ships to win.

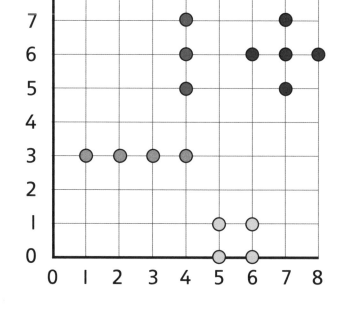

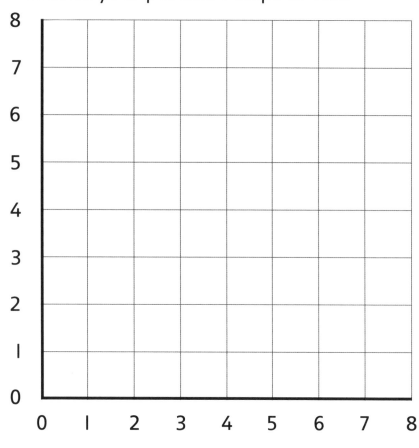

Allow each player to change the shape of one ship. The changed ship must have the same number of dots.

Notes

Published by Pearson Education Limited, 80 Strand, London, WC2R 0RL.

www.pearsonschools.co.uk

Text © Pearson Education Limited 2018, 2023
Edited by Pearson and Florence Production Ltd
First edition edited by Pearson, Little Grey Cells Publishing Services and Haremi Ltd
Designed and typeset by Pearson and PDQ Digital Media Solutions Ltd
First edition designed and typeset by Kamae Design
Original illustrations © Pearson Education Limited 2018, 2023
Illustrated by Laura Arias, John Batten, Fran and David Brylewski, Diego Diaz, Nigel Dobbyn, Virginia Fontanabona, Adam Linley and Nadene Naude at Beehive Illustration; Emily Skinner at Graham-Cameron Illustration; and Kamae Design
Images: The Royal Mint, 1971, 1982, 1990, 1992, 1998, 2017, 2023: 29–33, 34, 36, 38, 40–42, 44, 46; Bank of England: 29, 31–33, 35, 37, 39, 41, 43, 45, 47
Cover design by Pearson Education Ltd
Front and back cover illustrations by Diego Diaz and Nadene Naude at Beehive Illustration

Series editor: Tony Staneff
Lead author: Josh Lury
Consultants (first edition): Professor Liu Jian and Professor Zhang Dan

The rights of Tony Staneff and Josh Lury to be identified as authors of this work have been asserted by them in accordance with the Copyright, Designs and Patents Act 1988.

First published 2018
This edition first published 2023

27 26 25 24 23
10 9 8 7 6 5 4

British Library Cataloguing in Publication Data
A catalogue record for this book is available from the British Library

ISBN 978 1 292 41947 3

Printed in the UK by Bell & Bain Ltd, Glasgow

For Power Maths resources go to
www.activelearnprimary.co.uk

Note from the publisher
Pearson has robust editorial processes, including answer and fact checks, to ensure the accuracy of the content in this publication, and every effort is made to ensure this publication is free of errors. We are, however, only human, and occasionally errors do occur. Pearson is not liable for any misunderstandings that arise as a result of errors in this publication, but it is our priority to ensure that the content is accurate. If you spot an error, please do contact us at resourcescorrections@pearson.com so we can make sure it is corrected.